Evelyn Francis Capel:
A Celebration of a
Pioneering Spirit

Evelyn Capel, 1992 (photo: William Bishop).

Evelyn Francis Capel: A Celebration of a Pioneering Spirit

General Editor Rudolf Kirst

TEMPLE LODGE
London

Temple Lodge Publishing
51 Queen Caroline Street
London W6 9QL

Published by Temple Lodge 1997

A catalogue record for this book is available from the British Library

ISBN 0 904693 93 7

Cover by S. Gulbekian. Photo by Juliet van Otteren
Typesetting by Clare Crawford
Printed and bound in Great Britain by Cromwell Press Limited, Broughton Gifford, Wiltshire

Contents

Preface   7

A Prayer for The Christian Community   9

Acknowledgements   10

Introduction   11

Cecelia Fisher's Tribute   13

Early Days   23

Temple Lodge   37

A New Church   57

Help and Guidance   66

Sacraments   91

Pioneering   102

Books and Publishing   117

Personal Tributes   123

Appendix I: Chronology and Profile   168

Appendix II: Evelyn Francis Capel's
  Writings   172

Index of Contributors   175

Preface

The idea of inviting tributes to celebrate the life and work of Evelyn Francis Capel, priest of The Christian Community (London West) at Temple Lodge, was conceived to give people a means of expressing their appreciation and gratitude. At the same time, we decided to collate these letters for others to share. This initiative was also designed as a gesture of support for Evelyn as she meets the difficulties of her retirement from fifty-six years of service as a priest, and of her withdrawal from the centre that she had founded and developed as a cultural and religious centre with so much dedication for over thirty years.

The response to our appeal letter has been overwhelming in its warmth and encouragement. This book stands as a living witness to the wish of individuals to give something back to Evelyn. A few voices have been raised saying that tributes are best paid to the dead and not the living, but we believe that gratitude and support are due to a valued individual here and now.

Evelyn's life is mirrored back to her in these pages through the eyes of over a hundred people, and what beautiful pictures there are for her to behold! She has been uplifted by this experience and is deeply grateful for this gift, which friends from fourteen countries in five continents have given to her. She is equally grateful to the friend who has conveyed the contents of these letters to her – see Acknowledgments, page 10.

The completed book contains every letter sent to us that was relevant to our appeal, edited where necessary, but still preserving the original voices: a kaleidoscope of personal impressions and views.

At a recent synod (October 1997) of the priests of The

Christian Community in the UK, held at Temple Lodge – the centre Evelyn founded – the gathering formally expressed its appreciation for all the work that Evelyn has accomplished for the movement over the years, and sent good thoughts to her for the future. Similar expressions of thanks have been received from the international leadership of The Christian Community and from many of her colleagues abroad.

We warmly thank all the contributors and commend this book to Evelyn's friends and those connected with the movement that she represents. These letters may also appeal to those who recognise that Evelyn's work has a universal application and to those who are religious and spiritual seekers.

The Editing Team
October 1997

Note: Evelyn now lives at the Raphael Medical Centre in Hildenborough near Tonbridge, Kent, where she is well cared for in an anthroposophical setting.

A Prayer for The Christian Community *

Revd Evelyn Francis Capel

Offered to Christ
To let His Light shine on Earth

We Pray
That the light may shine truly
That it be not shadowed
That it be not deflected
That our hearts may guard it in truth.

We Pray
That the light of ideals
May shine stronger than the power
of organisation enforced by money.

May the ideal of freedom
Glow with respect in each heart
more strongly than the longing to dominate.
May the dignity of each one
Be felt within us
As we find the grace of Christ.

* From the Temple Lodge programme, Lent/Easter 1995.

Acknowledgements

One acknowledgement has to come before all others. Without Isla Bourke's personal sacrifice, untiring determination and hard work this book would not have come about. It was also Isla who, with endless patience, shared the many letters with Evelyn on her fortnightly visits over the past six months; at the time of writing this process still continues.

Warm thanks go to John Hugo who helped with the editing assisted by Fiona Tweedale. Ann Walsh gave unfailing support with the translations from the German and Gillian Waters useful tips in this respect. Dorothy Percival had a splendid linguistic input. Cecelia Fisher, Peter Heathfield, John Lees and Nelson Willby were always ready with ideas and advice. Margaret Jonas supplied information from the Library at Rudolf Steiner House, London. Stella Parton and Michael Beaumont clarified the details of Evelyn's literary output. Thomas Koeller offered a great deal of publishing advice. Eileen Simon generously provided practical assistance. Clare Crawford undertook the arduous task of typesetting and further editing and Sevak Gulbekian accepted the responsibility of publishing the book.

Sincere thanks to all who have financially supported this venture – about eighty individuals.

RK, September 1997

Introduction

Evelyn Francis Capel was called to further the work of The Christian Community, a movement for the renewal of Christianity, and the teachings of Rudolf Steiner, in many parts of the world. She pursued her vision with deep inner commitment and sacrifice, putting her outstanding personal gifts at the service of her mission.

Evelyn was the first British woman priest in The Christian Community.* Ordained in 1939, she was probably the first British woman ever to celebrate the Eucharist, fully incorporating the transubstantiation. In the grim years of 1939–45 Evelyn travelled to many parts of the UK, including Scotland, to build up centres of The Christian Community. In 1946 she radiated hope and encouragement to many shattered communities in Germany, which had suffered persecution during the Second World War. She founded The Christian Community (London West), first at Benen House, Chelsea, and then at Temple Lodge in Hammersmith. Between 1962 and 1965 Evelyn laid the first foundations of The Christian Community in South Africa and later brought the new rituals to Ghana, Zimbabwe, Portugal and other countries.

The world was Evelyn's parish. When she was called to celebrate a sacrament, she would follow that call, even if this meant long travels and hardships.

Wherever she went, at home or abroad, she sowed the seeds of Christian renewal, be it for the individual's inner life or for the beginning of new spiritual and social impulses.

Temple Lodge, the centre of The Christian Community (London West), was like a missionary station where every-

* For a detailed chronology of Evelyn's life, see Appendix I.

one, young or old, able or less able, visitors from near and
far were spiritually and physically nourished. Buzzing with
activity, it was also the hub of global initiatives. This included the writing and publishing of books that promoted
the culture of renewal.

Evelyn was a gateway for many people to find their way
to a new perception of Christianity and to anthroposophy.
Hers was a pioneering life throughout. May her priestly
spirit shine as a bright beacon into the future.

The contributions to the book are grouped under obvious
headings to give the publication a recognisable shape. The
tribute of Cecelia Fisher comes first in honour of her long
and faithful service to Evelyn. This is followed by the light-
hearted recollections of her fellow students (1937–39) at the
priests' seminary in Stuttgart, and accounts relating to war
and postwar years, hence Early Days (Chapter 2). The
reader is then led to the developments at Temple Lodge
(Chapter 3) and Evelyn's vision of 'A New Church' (Chapter 4). Help and Guidance (Chapter 5) gives an insight into
the dedication, wisdom and humanity shown by Evelyn to
those who approached her with life questions, whilst the
section on Sacraments (Chapter 6) leads us to the inner
sanctuary of the rituals. Pioneering (Chapter 7) introduces
the dynamics of her worldwide consciousness, and Books
and Publishing (Chapter 8) highlights her creative and penetrating thought processes. The final section, Personal Tributes (Chapter 9), is the largest with thirty-eight letters
rounding off the book.

Stella Parton and
Rudolf Kirst
September 1997

CHAPTER 1

Cecelia Fisher's Tribute

I am writing this tribute as someone who has been helping Evelyn in various roles – secretary, treasurer and trustee – since the establishment of The Christian Community (London West) at Benen House, Chelsea, in the early fifties.

Shortly after the Second World War, I attended a conference of The Christian Community at Albrighton Hall near Shrewsbury. It was there that I first met Evelyn Francis, as she then was, in rather an unusual way. It was at 6.45 a.m. on the staircase, as I waited to get into the bathroom. She introduced herself as Evelyn Francis and said she did not know me. I replied that, although not a member, I had come with a member of the Anthroposophical Society who was deeply interested in The Christian Community. Evelyn's last words to me outside the bathroom were: 'Whatever happens, please don't gossip in the bedroom because you must be in time for the 8.00 a.m. service. Otherwise you may not have room to sit down.' I thought this was rather startling, but when we got there I realised how lucky we were to get seats; there were about eighty people present.

The service – the Act of Consecration of Man – had a stunning effect on me, never to be forgotten. It took place in a large ballroom in the house and it was most impressive to see eight priests, including Evelyn, four on each side of the altar. Dr Heidenreich, the leader of The Christian Community in the UK, came in carrying the Eucharist. With him were two servers, one ringing a silver bell and the other carrying a Bible and the service book.

On the Sunday afternoon there were lots of jobs to be allocated, and Dr Heidenreich then gave an introductory talk.

All the other priests gave talks as well. Members could choose which study groups they wished to attend. I chose Evelyn's, and she was so interesting that I attended most of her meetings during the conference. My friend had asked her if I could join The Christian Community and she said, 'Leave it to me.' The day before the end of the conference she came up to my room, sat on the bed opposite me and said, 'It has been very nice meeting you. We would like to feel we have convinced you that you should become a member. You have been under observation; we have looked at your life situation, and we are all quite certain that you should do so. So tomorrow morning, Stanley Drake and I will have a little meeting with you in the chapel after the service to accept you as a member.' After returning to London I joined the Anthroposophical Society as well. That introduction to Evelyn, and to Dr Steiner's approach to Christianity, altered my outlook on life and has helped me to face very sad events during the years that have followed.

The early days of The Christian Community came from meetings at 1001 Finchley Road, near Golders Green, where Dr Heidenreich was resident. In the early fifties (after the sale of both '1001' and Albrighton Hall), he wanted to come and live at the Christian Community centre at 34 Glenilla Road, Belsize Park, and expected Evelyn to go to Bristol to open up a church there. It was a shock to Evelyn that she was expected to move out, considering that she had helped acquire the site, build up the congregation and hold the fort during and after the war – as ratepayer, secretary, trustee. Naturally she did not want to leave London and the congregation, and there were many members who did not want her to go. When told to leave, she collapsed and was cared for by a member of the congregation. It was at that point that Evelyn's supporters decided that Glenilla Road would be London North and that they would look for a another centre and call it London West or London South.

During those days at Glenilla Road, Evelyn first met Samuel Derry, who was connected with Steiner House. He had always been a great admirer of hers and befriended her at this difficult time, as did others. I remember her marriage to Derry – she refused to call him Samuel – forty-five years ago. It was a very happy day.

While we were looking for a new centre, one of our rich members offered us a beautiful flat in Grosvenor Square. Dr Heidenreich came and said it was a satisfactory place in which to hold Sunday services and blessed the property. Evelyn had also held services in an empty shop, its windows screened from public view by a curtain.

Then, in 1954, Colonel and Mrs Innes – she was in the congregation – offered us the whole of the lower part of their house at 34 Draycott Place, Chelsea. They said we could live there rent-free, provided we could supply someone to attend to the central heating for the whole house. We never paid a penny! We called the property Benen House, after St Benen, St Patrick's dearest disciple and eventually his successor. There were large rooms in the basement where we could gather, have meals and hold events. And a huge ballroom above became the lovely chapel, with a bedroom next door. Colonel and Mrs Innes and their children moved to the upper floors. It was a wonderful gesture on their part. The congregation followed Evelyn to Benen House, in spite of difficult journeys, and Derry would wait until the last person was in before closing the door.

We always knew that Benen House was a temporary arrangement and that we had to look for something more permanent. The efforts of Derry and Mrs Margaret McDougall were indefatigable, as we started to look for a suitable property. Derry, helped by a member of the Anthroposophical Society, arranged for us to buy a Georgian house in Hammersmith – Temple Lodge, 51 Queen Caroline Street. It had once been the home of the artist Sir Frank Brangwyn, who had built a 'modern' extension as a studio, later turned into the Christian Community chapel. The house, which belonged to a builder, was in a poor condition. There was a lot of the builder's rubble, and the main staircase had been damaged by bombs, so you could not go upstairs.

A dedicated group of members raised the money to buy

THE CHRISTIAN COMMUNITY
London West

BENEN HOUSE,
34, DRAYCOTT PLACE, SLOANE SQUARE, LONDON S.W.3.
KENSINGTON 9843.

Programme
for
Lent and Easter 1957

The Act of Consecration of Man is celebrated
each Thursday at 11-0 a.m.
each Sunday   at 11-0 a.m.

Four sermons in Lent preceding the Act of Consecration of Man at 11-0 a.m.

1st Sunday March 24th :   Adam and Jesus
2nd Sunday March 31st :   Melchisedek and the Messiah
3rd Sunday April 7th :   Moses and the Redeemer
4th Sunday April 14th :   Abraham and the King of the Jews

Facsimile of programme from Benen House.

Temple Lodge and two registered charities were formed: The Benen Trust, which owned the property, and The Christian Community (London West), which administered it.

Evelyn finally moved into Temple Lodge in 1961. Sadly, Derry had died shortly before this, having developed cancer. In those days the chapel was in what is now the library, and the library was directly above. Evelyn camped in the room alongside the chapel, while repairs were going on all around her. One of the members gave her a bed-settee and someone else gave her a beautiful desk.

Evelyn carried out the instructions of Rudolf Steiner that, if you really wanted to be a priest, you had to start from scratch with meetings in a private house. Then, when you had sufficient support, you could build a chapel.

When Evelyn married Bert Capel in October 1967, he suggested that the first and second floors, above what was then the chapel, should be turned into bedrooms in which we could put people up. Various members from all parts of the world have lived in the house over the years. This has helped to cover the running costs of Temple Lodge.

Evelyn had wonderful support from her four sisters. Edith had been a hospital sister in Singapore and had been taken prisoner by the Japanese during the Second World War. She helped run Temple Lodge and worked in the garden, where she used to talk to the plants. Janet had been a supervisor in a women's prison in the north before becoming an inspector of approved schools for girls. She lived in Chelsea and when she retired she bought a house at Windsor so that she could still be near enough to help at Temple Lodge. She came every Sunday to prepare the lunch and gave Evelyn many gifts, including a beautiful hexagonal table for the Blue Room and a lovely carpet for the hall. Janet's twin sister, Joyce, lived in Cheltenham and her children attended Wynstones Rudolf Steiner school. Win took a great interest in Temple Lodge, even though she lived in Scotland. Personally I feel very strongly connected with this family. I think I knew them in the past and that we have been brought together again in this incarnation.

Apart from her priestly duties in London, Evelyn received many calls for help from people in distress from all over the country, including road accident victims and potential suicides. These calls often came in the middle of the night, and Evelyn had no hesitation in rising from her bed to do her best to help them.

She allowed Narcotics Anonymous to meet at Temple Lodge and to use the dining room during the day. She held meetings to help mothers bring up their children. Evelyn would talk to the mothers while they were having their lunch and three or four of them had their babies christened by her. Three of us who had good voices used to sing in harmony; it charmed the babies and kept them quiet. Evelyn encouraged Mrs Wreford to develop a playgroup at Temple Lodge, which lasted several years.

When there were several children in the congregation, a special service was held for them after lunch. Evelyn would expect us to come to the service to support the children. The service was followed by a party for them, with drinks and cakes. Lots of activities for children took place at Temple Lodge, including a hunt for eggs at Easter and greenery on the floor in a spiral pattern at Advent, when apples were prepared with candles in the middle. The children would take these into the spiral to be lit from the central candle and, on the outward journey, place them on the floor amid the greenery, representing the light of the new Christian year. Evelyn conducted plays at various times of the year in which both children and adults could take part. It was enormous fun diving into the wardrobe, pulling out various garments and deciding what we should wear according to the season of the year. Evelyn eventually published a book of these plays (*Collected Plays for Young and Old*).

I remember Evelyn's wonderful musical events on Sunday afternoons. Lady Dorothy Pratt would hire a minibus to bring along students and they would play lovely music. People naturally put their contributions in a bowl and this raised money for The Christian Community. Ian Houston, the musician, and Dr Ralph Twentyman, the homoeopath,

Evelyn (bottom), aged six, with her sisters (from top) Winifred, Edith, Janet and Joyce.

Evelyn (second row, far left) at Pate's Grammar School, Cheltenham.

Evelyn (directly below the centre pillar) at Somerville College, Oxford, first-year intake photograph, 1929.

often came to Temple Lodge; so did Sir George Trevelyan,*
who gave wonderful talks on Aquarius and the future according to Rudolf Steiner. They all refused payment. I recall
Evelyn and Sir George sharing a platform at Olympia. Afterwards Sir George said, 'Well done! It is an honour to
share a platform with you, Evelyn.' And we mustn't forget
the opportunities we had of practising eurythmy in the
charge of Michael Beaumont and others.

On one of her Sunday afternoon talks Evelyn discovered
that most of us were struggling with Dr Steiner's *The Philosophy of Spiritual Activity*.‡ She was amazed at this and decided we must have a week when we were all in the house
together and she would take us through the *Philosophy*. It
was so successful that she carried out this particular study-
week every year. In the afternoons, as a break, we were able
to join Audrey Bayfield's painting lessons and there were
opportunities to visit various museums and art galleries.
Then, in the evenings, those who were staying in the house
had another little talk. Many of us returned again and
again, and Evelyn said, 'I shall be glad to know when you
reach saturation point.'

Evelyn never boasted about her intellectual achievements, in spite of a degree in modern history from Somerville College, Oxford in 1932. And records show that, when
she attended Pate's Grammar School for Girls in Cheltenham, she was first on the list for all England in the 1926
School Certificate examinations! One of her sisters is reput-
ed to have said, 'Thank goodness we've only got one blue-

---

* Sir George Trevelyan, Bt, MA, was Warden of the Shropshire Adult
College at Attingham Park from 1948 to 1971 and founder of the
Wrekin Trust, an organisation launched to run courses on spiritual subjects all over the country. He lectured worldwide on such subjects as
'Spiritual Awakening in our Time' and wrote a number of books, including the trilogy, *A Vision of the Aquarian Age*, *Operation Redemption*
and *Exploration into God*. He met anthroposophy in the 1930s and was
to repeat many times that this changed his life. He became something
of a father figure within the so-called New Age movement.

‡ Contributors use both titles, either *The Philosophy of Spiritual Activity* or
The Philosophy of Freedom.

stocking in the family.' (Apparently their mother expected the sisters to wait on Evelyn so that she could spend all her time studying.)

Evelyn was in great demand all over the world. Temple Lodge suffered until she came back, although we were fortunate to have other colleagues step in when she was away. Evelyn has been a wonderful influence on all who have come into contact with her, and has had an everlasting effect on the spiritual side of all our lives.

July 1997

CHAPTER 2

Early Days

Revd Jan Dostal

Prague, Czech Republic (translation coordinated by the editor)

My memories of Evelyn Capel reach back more than half a century. During the Second World War, The Christian Community in Prague had been prohibited by the Nazis, a fact that made me even more determined to become a priest. The end of the war had come and I had to ask myself where I wanted to have my training. Stuttgart was the obvious choice and also the nearest centre. But Stuttgart had been bombed and also, for political reasons after the collapse of the Nazi regime, it would have been impossible to undertake a course of studies there.

I had a fair knowledge of English, which I zealously tried to perfect. I got hold of old copies of *The Christian Community*. I delved into these and also tried to memorise specific items. Then I came across an article, 'Fra Angelico Now' [January 1936], by a certain Evelyn Francis. This impressed me deeply and it suddenly brought to life a great interest in Fra Angelico's pictures. And I wondered what this lady who wrote the article, and who could so infectiously put across a feeling for the delicacy of the colours, might look like.

At the end of March 1946 I was at last able to ring the doorbell at Glenilla Road. Two ladies answered, names were mentioned, but in my excitement I did not take them in. But one made me immediately feel, 'There she is!' And so she was. At that time she lived at Glenilla Road, as I would from then on. That evening I was already able to attend a study group on *The Philosophy of Freedom*, which she took in her room. There was a picture in the room, the head of Christ as carved by Steiner as part of his huge statue. A thought occurred to me – childish perhaps, odd I realised – but it persisted: it seemed that Evelyn's countenance was in harmony with that of the Christ. This confirmed my conviction: you can confidently rely on this human being to pass on to you the right and reliable impulses. This confidence has been fully confirmed in the course of time.

I came from an actor's family, recited well and with pleasure and also enjoyed acting. My training as a seminarist also included a course in speech formation, which took place at Glenilla Road. I enjoyed this and I tried to carry out the exercises as well as possible. But then, one day, Evelyn called me to her. She said – quietly but firmly – 'You cannot continue to handle language in this way.' It upset and confused me. How come? 'You are treating the language as something external. An actor may speak like that but not a priest. You must learn to speak from the heart, from the ego.' I knew she was right. But when it comes to it, how does one do that, speak from the heart? Evelyn then took on my training in speech formation. A search began for an entirely new source of speech, also a battle with my own speech organism and its habits. This was not simply a task for weeks or months. It was a lifelong task. In fact, I am still tackling it today, after half a century. But what would have happened if Evelyn had not intervened?

I cannot remember ever having heard Evelyn preaching morality or laying down laws for the lives of others. But again and again I heard her say to me, 'You must try to live out of your future ego.' The future ego: that is an ideal to which one aspires, but of its existence one can already be inwardly aware. It should ever more become the source, the impulse to human action.

As the year of my study in England was soon to come to its end, I was asked by a small group to talk about twentieth-century music (I was a qualified musician). Although I

Back row (left to right): Samuel Derry, Dr Emil Bock, Anne Phillips.
Front row: Evelyn, Mavis Metcalfe, Dorothy Hegg and Grottfried
Husemann.

Evelyn with a family in Freiburg, Germany, with whom she stayed in
order to learn German (around 1935).

spoke fairly good English at the time, I found it very difficult to put the theme across clearly. I prepared the talk conscientiously. Afterwards I was thanked and appreciation
was expressed. Evelyn was also present but did not say
anything. So I went to her and asked whether she had liked
the talk. She seemed somewhat embarrassed and then said,
'You know, Jan, you are obviously gifted as a teacher to
teach others. Only, as a priest, one should not in the first
place be a teacher; in the first place one must be a brother.'
You can imagine how I felt. But again I had been given a
word for all my life, perhaps even for more than one life.

I was ordained in Prague. During the three years of my
activity there before The Christian Community was once
again prohibited (this time by the Communists), I had to
overcome many inner weaknesses and difficulties – my
training had really been too short. Much developed quite
differently from what I had envisaged. The only person to
whom I could appeal as a counsellor was again Evelyn. Letters were exchanged between Prague and London. Every
time Evelyn patiently tried to enlighten me, to strengthen,
to console. I felt: you may be working in Prague but the
source of your inner strength, which does not let you give
up, pours forth again and again from England.

Then outer circumstances interrupted our contact, but
the strengthening memories and the gratitude for what has
been experienced remain. All this cannot be extinguished.

Revd Franz-Heinrich Himstedt
Pforzheim, Germany (translation coordinated by the editor)

Being at the priests' seminary of The Christian Community
in Stuttgart from 1936 to 1939 was a memorable time for our
group – the new important professional commitment, meeting lecturers, living with the ritual, created an underlying
hopeful mood for our common studies. It was moving to
get to know fellow students, to experience something of
their destiny and the path that brought them to The Christian Community. Amongst them, the three from England

soon gained our sympathy. Something of the wider world seemed to waft around when the English language resounded through the house.

As non-Germans, the British had to get used to some aspects of our way of life, a fact that we natives only realised when occasionally a remark broke through their natural reserve. Often it concerned trifles but they added up. There was no lack of care in the well-kept, newly built seminary, but they faced what was to them unusual. Why, for example, such an early start to the day, and why the concentrated and exhausting sequence of courses? Patiently taking part in the joint exercises in speech formation (which students were expected to continue in private in their rooms) proved wearisome for the British. But our friends got used to things and gradually slipped into the routine, experiencing progress of soul and spirit towards their future priesthood.

Miss Evelyn Francis, Stanley Drake and Kenneth Walsh were popular and respected among the fellow seminarists, and the intensive study soon turned us into a friendly community. The service at the beginning of the day was followed by theological and scientific courses, speech formation and eurythmy, as well as sharing in practical work in the house and garden. And there were the little outings. We climbed a hill, allowed our thoughts to wander into the future, raised the view into spiritual heights and wondered whither the folk spirit might soon send one or the other. We might also leave the higher spheres and come down to chat about what the wayside presented – asked for the English names of flowers we gave them in German. It was not difficult to engage Evelyn in conversation, and it did not bother her when, in her refreshing way, she got the pronunciation of a number of German words wrong or was answered in even worse English. We talked about the courses given in the morning – also of the difficult exercises in speech formation!

Evelyn commented on these educational exertions with humour and equanimity and, during one of the outings, she gave us the difficult story of the two toads of Tidsbury. She

enjoyed our keenness to get it right. She assisted us patiently across the complicated linguistic hurdles of this
well-known English alliterative verse. (Two toads – totally
tired – trying to trot – to Tidsbury.) Her humorous acting
talent was clearly evident. And soon some of us had, near
enough, achieved repeating the obstacle course of the tired
toads faultlessly and as quickly as possible. What a good
counterfoil to the seminary's 'pfiffich pfeifenden Pferden'!

Humour proved to be Evelyn's faithful helper in over-
coming many obstacles she had to face in her life. It is this
little scene during a walk in Swabia that presents itself to
me as if wrapped in sunlight whenever I think of the early
recollections that bind me to the revered priestly being of
Evelyn Capel.

Revd Wilhelm Hoerner
Esslingen, Germany (translation coordinated by the editor)

Five recollections of Evelyn Francis at the priests' seminary
in Stuttgart during 1938/39

1. We had been on a walking tour of the Schwäbische Alb
and had got completely lost. Our small group of seminarists
had walked unconcerned and without aim. When finally
nobody knew the right way any longer, Evelyn turned em-
phatically to me and said, 'Wilhelm, you must lead so that
we have a Fuhrer and we can grumble if things go wrong.'
The word *Führer* at the time was fully appropriated by the
man in Berlin. Evelyn pronounced it with 'u' (oo). This English version was a surprise to us all and quite new.

2. Evelyn always wanted to learn to speak good German
and also spoke with people on the tram. Once she came into
the seminary kitchen and asked, 'What is this? To let one
go?' It referred to passing wind.

3. At the time there was on the Charlottenplatz in Stuttgart a kind of museum about Germans abroad. In it was a
large display that compared in small and large circles the
total space occupied by Germany with the total space covered by the then British Empire: a small circle and an enormous one. And when the students wanted to tease each

other, their hands would form a small and a big 'L' as in eurythmy. Once, at dinner, Evelyn asked for the potatoes. Before passing them on, the student concerned first made a small and a big 'L', referring to the display. Evelyn was deeply offended, threw knife and fork down, had two beautiful pearly tears in her blue eyes and shouted at the top of her voice, 'I am not English, I am a Celt.' And with that she left the dining room.

4. I had invited Evelyn to my home. At night my mother took her to the guest room. Shortly after, Evelyn asked my mother to come with her once more. At that time one still slept between two huge feather-filled duvets. Pointing to what seemed an odd bed to her, Evelyn asked, 'At what level do I get in?'

5. We visited Rothenburg on the Tauber. Ahead of us, English was being spoken loudly. I said to Evelyn, 'Listen – your compatriots.' She stopped, her eyes piercing me excitedly, and shouted, 'Fie, Wilhelm, fie. They are not English, they are American.' I was neither conscious of the linguistic distinctions at the time, nor that equating the two was insulting to someone who now considered herself English, as against Celtic in the earlier story.

John Nightingale
Kings Langley, Hertfordshire, England

After the end of the Second World War I met and was enthused by some of the leaders and members of The Christian Community. On demobilisation I needed accommodation in London in order to complete my architectural training. Miss Evelyn Francis was at that time holding the fort at Glenilla Road, where she graciously accepted me.

Evelyn was already a priest and delighted to tell us of her experiences in her former career, serving as a waitress in a Lyons Corner Shop as part of her management training.

Dr Heidenreich, ever genial, appeared from time to time to bring peace and harmony. Evelyn was a volcano, determined to get things done and to get the Community moving. Once, to satisfy and impress officialdom, a meeting had to be arranged at short notice to fill the house with as many people as possible, so into the highways and byways we had to go, and what a motley assembly it was!

In the house was also a lady who liked her comforts. She was particularly put out by a broken pane of glass in the bathroom, which made it very cold and which Evelyn refused to have repaired, either on economy grounds or more on the insistence that it was good for the soul!

The house was held together by the love and care of Muriel Allen who, in the straitened circumstances of the times, always managed to produce a delicious evening meal, and all had to contend with the small inadequate kitchen. Another inmate was Miss Mavis Metcalfe, who was a lady of good intentions but who found it difficult to make up her mind, except that she thought it would be far better if I had some of the corners knocked off.

At the second Christmas after the war, we all went into the dining room at Glenilla Road, with Evelyn and the wireless, to listen to Clement Attlee giving his message to the nation. The expectation was that he would announce some extra rations, which we could then send to German Community friends in their distress, but it was not to be. Clement said there was scarcely enough for our needs and there would be nothing extra. Our faces fell.

I was a wayward inmate of the house with my own aims, which did not agree with the community Evelyn was trying to build. She knew in Kilburn a married couple with a daughter. They had risked their all to go fruit farming in Canada. They had lost everything and had had to return to this country. The wife was shattered. Evelyn recommended me to lodge with them, believing that, besides helping the finances, the need to prepare a proper breakfast and provide the evening meal would be helpful.

Evelyn told me that success in life has its dangers, but also of the great courage required to face failure.

Evelyn was always very keen on acting, on our becoming even for a little while something different, a new person in a

Evelyn with her first husband, Samuel Derry, attending a wedding.

new guise. With her we acted in 'The Shepherds' at Temple Lodge [from *Collected Plays for Young and Old*].

The move to the Kensington premises [Benen House] was a struggle, and later even greater the challenge of Temple Lodge, the history of which fascinated Evelyn. I remember days there with a measuring tape and schemes for a new chapel. I still carry a design for it, which she handed out to many to bear in their consciousness for the future.

I remember Dr Heidenreich once remarking that Evelyn did have some curious ideas. A favourite theme of hers was that birds with black and white plumage were definitely more evolved than, say, the brilliant kingfisher. I never did gather where the destructive magpie fitted in!

I remember Evelyn's first husband, Mr Derry. He was a quiet man, sweeping, cleaning, making all spick and span and attending to all her needs. He was devoted.

Evelyn lectured tirelessly. She was not a driver and in those days, to travel to different venues, she sometimes had to rely on taxis. Their drivers she found to be mines of information and considered them to be the salt of the earth.

I must say a word about her clear writing. Her books on the sacraments and the Christian year spring to mind.

In taking services, Evelyn was always forceful. I particularly remember a baptism at the Kings Langley Priory with a howling child throughout and Evelyn, in a determined voice, rising that all should hear, pressing on regardless. She also took the funeral service for Nathanial Bowron, teacher at the New School, Kings Langley, as it was then.

Not so long ago [1989] I was glad to be present at the celebration at Temple Lodge for the fifty years of Evelyn's work in the priesthood.

Anne Thomson
West Hoathly, West Sussex, England

I first knew Evelyn in the summer of 1943, introduced to her by Geordie Thomson (who later became my husband) at Glenilla Road. I cannot quite recall when Glenilla Road opened but I believe, with her realistic vision of the future, Evelyn was largely responsible for persuading Dr Heidenreich that this was a necessity in wartime London.

Evelyn was very beautiful facially when she was young, and she had her stubby choleric physical body too. Many people living at Glenilla Road were at that time in awe of her. She attracted a large number of young people to visit Glenilla Road, some in the Forces – the crowd who used to go to lectures at Rudolf Steiner House and to lectures on Dr Steiner elsewhere in London.

There was a tremendous interest in spiritual science in those days amongst the young (and many not so young). Many of the people who later became leading figures in various areas of anthroposophical life either stayed briefly at the house or visited Evelyn there.

I became inspired by The Christian Community and used to travel across London from Gloucester Road Tube station to Belsize Park to go to services conducted by Evelyn, Dr Heidenreich, Stanley Drake and Adam Bittleston. Even then, Evelyn's celebration of the Act of Consecration was outstanding but, following her various traumatic life experiences and personal development, it became altogether wonderful and inspiring. With her beautiful voice, perfect enunciation and ability to let the spiritual word flow directly through the vessel of her strong personality to the congregation, it became an important, sustaining and supportive spiritual experience. It became stronger over the years.

I remember two years running her producing some of the Oberufer Christmas plays, and I remember the wonderful midnight service at The Studio* one year, with a large Christmas tree and Communion celebrated at the Act of Consecration on 24/25 December. This of course was not entirely her 'show', but she took her part amongst other priests with grace and authority.

At that time, Florence cooked meals for the large number of visitors who came to see Evelyn in the afternoons and evenings. We used to have long, frank conversations about

---

* A Christian Community chapel in Maitland Park Villas, London NW3.

the war, pacifism, reincarnation, spiritual science, etc. I well remember a conversation about pacifism, which to me, as a physiotherapist, was important. Evelyn had of course spent years in Stuttgart before ordination and knew the Germans well. She had also experienced the rise of Hitler and Nazism. She had seen the incarnation of evil in the Third Reich and was convinced that the opposition of the Allied powers was a necessity and should have taken place much earlier. Her reasoning and vision seemed to me valid and certainly reversed my, at that time, rather wishy-washy pacifism.

I continued seeing her and going to the services until the summer of 1944. We became close and discussed the possibility of me becoming a priest. She believed that three of the people who came to see her were, or could be, suitable candidates, including myself and my subsequent husband.

This was the time of the flying bombs and later the V2s. I remember sitting in the front row of seats one Sunday during the Act of Consecration of Man, which Evelyn was taking, when there was the tremendous flash of light that always preceded a V2 (to which of course she paid no attention). I, on the other hand, counted the seconds before the explosion, to find out how far away it had come down. This was the bomb that damaged Selfridges.

Shortly after this I became pregnant. It was necessary to make up my mind what I should do. I had two developments for my career in mind – either to become a priest of The Christian Community or leave my profession, which I found frustrating, and become a doctor. But when I contemplated an abortion, although it was very early days, I could not bring myself to have it.

I then discussed the situation with Evelyn at some length. There was no question of marriage. After several discussions, she offered me accommodation at Glenilla Road during the pregnancy and I accepted the offer. My mother obtained money for me without having to tell my father why, and I moved up to Glenilla Road and let my flat.

I believe Evelyn's book *Pictures from the Apocalypse* is outstanding. Not only is it a true visionary exposition of the St

John's Revelation, it is also a wonderful picture of her own spiritual development.

To me, looking at Evelyn's life, which I have followed either closely in the early days, from a distance between 1947 and 1980, then in touch more closely and subsequently, fortuitously, much closer than I had envisaged, I can say, as will everyone else, that she is a truly remarkable woman. I believe she has been a voice for the future whose vision that anthroposophy and The Christian Community should live in the 'world' and that lectures and sermons should be given widely to those who are *not* anthroposophists or members of The Christian Community, has been crucial in spreading the 'word' during the fifty-three years I have known or been associated with her.

I attended a course on *The Philosophy of Freedom* given by Evelyn in 1984 or 1985. I still have the notes; the course was clear and clarified several difficult thoughts.

I admire and care very much for Evelyn. I believe that Rachael Shepherd, whom she chose to be her successor, will be well able to continue her work.

Evelyn, Prague, 1947.

Revd Walther Voigt

Dresden, Germany (translation coordinated by the editor)

I can add only a small piece to the tribute to our dear Evelyn Francis Capel.

One recollection goes back to the shared time at the priests' seminary in Stuttgart. Karin Haupt gave a lesson in speech formation. We had to recite a German poem that contained the word *Kauz*. Evelyn wanted to know the meaning of *Kauz*. In answer she was told that this is a small owl that hides in a hole in a tree during the day. At night, however, it silently hovers around hunting for mice and other nocturnal animals. Human beings who spin strange thoughts during the day and cannot relax during the night are also known by this name. After a moment of thought Evelyn turned to me saying, 'Mr Voigt, are you a *Kauz*?' We laughed merrily as this question came out of the blue.

Evelyn frequently offered comments spiked with imaginative humour. During afternoon tea, which was shared with Stanley Drake, Kenneth Walsh and Johannes Rath, we used to pull each others' legs during carefree conversations. On these occasions I was the person most predisposed to the theme of *Kauz*. We were good 'fellows', as one says in English.

We met again after many years in 1946. Much had to be rebuilt in The Christian Community. We were trying to arouse enthusiasm for new ideals during youth conferences. We were just in full swing on a large stage in a school hall in Rendsburg, north of Hamburg, when I, as organiser, was called away to meet an English lady announced as a VIP. There was Evelyn; what a joy! She had taken the first opportunity to find her German friends in the guise of a military colonel. At once she was on stage and greeted us cordially in beautifully spoken German. She stood before us as a herald of a new Europe, radiating hope for the future and a Christian humanity in Europe.

CHAPTER 3

Temple Lodge

Anon 1

Looking back over the years, I have observed that a number of people (myself included) spent an important section of their lives attending Temple Lodge, where they came under Evelyn Capel's influence. From her they received a great deal of anthroposophical knowledge during her lectures and courses and in private interviews. Evelyn used her excellent, clear, logical brain power to clarify – even simplify for me – some of the more difficult of Rudolf Steiner's lectures. Whilst giving public talks she had a very rare and enviable ability to assess her audience and adapt her lecture accordingly.

Evelyn's sympathetic attention to personal problems enabled many 'to go on' and to find their own personal path in life as anthroposophists.

Many of us wish to express our real gratitude to her for all her many years of work, often performed under personal stress and considerable practical difficulties.

Aban Bana
Bombay, India

When I think back on the seven years that I spent in London, one of the most important and outstanding personalities whom I encountered was Revd Evelyn Capel. She always welcomed me at Temple Lodge with open arms and a cheerful greeting. Although she was so busy, she always had time for me and took a great interest in my work. My class at the North London Rudolf Steiner School all loved her and her very special cat, Augusta. Evelyn accompanied my class when we went on a study tour of London, and we were all amazed at the great knowledge that she had of her beloved city.

Evelyn always allowed us to hold our meetings or give eurythmy performances at Temple Lodge. Discussions with her were always a great pleasure. She said the most lofty and profound things in such a clear and down-to-earth manner that the simplest among us understood.

When my elderly parents came to visit me from India, Evelyn welcomed them most hospitably and even arranged that we could go on a couple of country excursions with her. My parents remember her with great warmth and love.

I love Evelyn Capel, and I am very grateful to have met her and known her.

Audrey Bayfield
Manchester, England

I had recently retired from teaching art. Mrs Capel suggested, during a subsequent visit, that I should take a painting class at Temple Lodge, and this I did for a number of years, twice yearly, at Christmas and Easter, and sometimes in the summer.

To me Temple Lodge became a second home. It was unfailingly warm and welcoming and free. Evelyn and Bert Capel sacrificed personal privacy and comfort and put everything they had into the nurturing of what went on in that house. Temple Lodge was a centre to which people came from all over the world. The Act of Consecration of Man was the centre of that centre. No matter if many of the people one talked to at breakfast were not involved in that central activity, they were part of the whole, however fleetingly, and significant contacts were made between people of very different backgrounds. Everybody was welcome, as the signboard outside proclaimed. And those who took part

Evelyn's beloved cat, Augusta.

Evelyn with Augusta, 1992.

in the activities of Temple Lodge, the faithful congregation and those who came at festival times, were, I am sure, as enriched by their experiences as I was.

Yes, it was untidy, happy, sometimes unhappy, warm, never cold, never stinting or turning away, open. Oh, there were crises, but aren't there in every family? And it was a family to which I and others felt we belonged, and there was humour, and cups of tea in the kitchen, and freedom to be oneself. And at the centre of all this creative activity was Evelyn Capel and, until his untimely death, Bert Capel with his many-sided practical skills. It was a great adventure. Now it is over and something new must take its place. May the foundations, and the founder, never be forgotten.

John Campbell
Tarbert, Argyll, Scotland

I came in contact with Temple Lodge and Mrs Capel by accident while out walking in Hammersmith. A sign advertising 'Local honey for sale' caught my eye and I ventured in to investigate. I got talking to the assistant, and when I mentioned I was a beekeeper his eyes lit up and I was taken to meet Mrs Capel.

You might say my arrival at Temple Lodge was all down to divine intervention. As Mrs Capel had recently lost her husband, who had looked after the bees, and I had just returned to London from a spell in Canada working for a commercial beekeeper, I was invited to look after the bees and I had no hesitation in accepting.

My regular summer visits brought me in contact with Mrs Capel who always took a keen interest in the bees and what they were doing.

While I was away working a well-intentioned 'stand-in' stirred up the bees, which led to a small girl on the council estate over the wall being badly stung. Her irate father came round and put his fist through a glass front door panel. He calmed down only when Mrs Capel gave him some of our honey as a peace offering.

Although I never witnessed it, Mrs Capel and friends always chanted a rhyme to the bees on New Year's Day*. She was also very insistent that the bees be managed according to the principles laid down by Rudolf Steiner. Through my visits to Temple Lodge I met a lot of very nice people and gained a superficial understanding of the Anthroposophical Society and The Christian Community.

* Bees, Bees of Paradise
  Do the Work of Jesus Christ
  Do the Work that no Man can.

Judith Da Deppo
Domegge, Dolomiten, Italy

I have known Evelyn since 1980 and have a karma with her, which I know will endure well into the future. I have written down thoughts written by Rudolf Steiner on Goethe's poem of Christmas and Easter.* The thoughts explain what I have found in Temple Lodge and through knowing Evelyn and the members of The Christian Community and Anthroposophical Society.

The spirit of Christianity more profound which an individual finds in that establishment [Temple Lodge] is expressed in the cross surrounded by roses and now the pilgrim who enters becomes really welcomed by such a spirit.

As soon as the individual enters he/she is fully aware that, in this house, this or that religion of the world does not dominate. But a higher unity of the religions of the world dominates.

The individual recognises a direct connection with the star that conducted the three holy kings and with its significance. That star, which has a permanent significance, opens the path towards consciousness of self, the dedication of self, and self perfecting. It is the path which opens comprehension for the gifts received by the Danish King in dreams, the star which appears at the birth of every mature being and welcomes in the self the principle (principio) Christ.

* This item is from *The Mysteries – A Christmas and Easter Poem by Goethe* (a lecture by Rudolf Steiner, Cologne, 25 December 1907, published in English by Mercury Press, Spring Valley, NY, USA, 1987). The contributor has translated it herself and interspersed it with her own comments.

The soul transforms its connections in ideas and thoughts, then develops in the soul health forces, through which the soul can activate (work) in the world regeneration.

In these principles (ideas) man can alone find peace and contentment in the proper Monserrat [which word I understand to be the entering of Parsifal in the Grail and living in its benediction and in the castle].

Personally, I feel and think that Evelyn has contributed to a furtherance of anthroposophy and The Christian Community because her spirit is working among the younger generation and in unlikely places. I have a great, great hope for the future. I see it as a Celtic future.

A word more personally on Evelyn and the members of The Christian Community of Temple Lodge. I am a late developer and at no time did I find any form of snobbery. In real/ideal terms I found encouragement, love and understanding, and much light conversation.

Ruth Donnithorne
London, England

I don't really know consciously how Evelyn has helped me with the solving of life questions; I only know that I always felt much better in her presence.

With regard to precarious life situations, I very rarely came to see Evelyn for consultation, but I always felt much strengthened when I came to Temple Lodge. The cheerful way in which she ran Temple Lodge always made me feel a lot better, so that life became worthwhile again for me. Also, with my mother's severe and difficult illness and my father always spending so much time at his work, she was a real stabiliser in my life.

I very rarely asked Evelyn philosophical questions. I thought it best just to allow her talks and conversation to sink in, so to speak, so that in this way I got some of the answers to these questions. It was better for me to listen so that I got *some* answers. I cannot say that I achieved more than this.

I found Evelyn's cheerful manner very healing. One could really go by what she said, and thus the spiritual struggle became less, thus helping my inner soul. So therefore I could relax more.

I suffer from paralysis and arthritis, though this may not be apparent. I also had a serious accident at the impressionable age of twenty-one years. Physically I have always felt Evelyn's care bringing healing to my body, with also the services and her talks to help me. Mentally I felt stimulated by her talks and her person; these enabled me to cope with my problems.

The affection with which Evelyn performed the rituals of the Act of Consecration of Man for humanity was very apparent. Many babies were also christened by Evelyn Capel at Temple Lodge.

As far as the furtherance of anthroposophy and The Christian Community is concerned, I only know that Evelyn has immensely and greatly influenced people along these lines. In The Christian Community she is known and greatly respected and has done invaluable work in the renewal of Christianity, which she so very much believes in.

Michael Drummond
Nottingham, England

I met anthroposophy at the age of twenty-eight. I attended the 1975 Sheffield conference of the society with Sir George Trevelyan's Wrekin Trust. Whilst there I also met The Christian Community, as I was invited to join a small group visiting the Community House to take part in the Act of Consecration of Man. My path led from here to the door of Temple Lodge.

Temple Lodge became my 'second home' for nearly seven years. I would arrive for the service every Sunday and stay until the last cup of tea in the afternoon. I loved the special atmosphere – one, I felt, in which each member of the congregation was valued but allowed the freedom to participate as each felt able; it was supportive without being intrusive. The free association and mutual interest of those gathered on those Sundays was a complement to the deepening spiritual life brought to me through the ritual.

Age or background was irrelevant to this friendship; we were all on a journey of discovery into the meaning of Christ in our lives. And so remarkably jolly!

This was something Evelyn herself helped to engender through her humour and sense of fun. Her afternoon talks were full of amusing stories and anecdotes based on a keen observation of human nature and the different folk souls.

Although these visits to Temple Lodge were like a breath of fresh air in my life, I fairly soon had an opportunity to become more involved. 'How about serving?' Evelyn asked one Sunday. Characteristically, this wasn't so much an invitation to learn but to do, learning by my mistakes (which were well tolerated). This learning process coincided with the movement of the chapel out of the house and into the studio. As conversion work was carried out, our chapel position and vestry kept moving, so I had to be versatile.

Evelyn also found out that I was interested in the stars. I was invited to talk after the service in the mornings, on Sunday afternoons, and to share duties on a Keswick conference. This en-*courage*-ment from Evelyn helped me to gain the confidence to speak in public and to learn that I needed to be constantly in tune with my interest. I might be asked to stand up and speak at the drop of a hat! I eventually ended up writing star notes for *The Threshing Floor** for a number of years.

After nearly seven years of working with anthroposophy, I felt a need to make a career change and moved to Ilkeston to teach. However, things did not work out as I anticipated and I had to leave my post, which happened coincidentally with my marriage. On visiting London, I remember explaining the circumstances to Evelyn, perhaps expecting a sympathetic response. 'Remember that freedom is the other side of failure,' she said with a smile. This aphorism proved to be just right as it helped me to face up to this failure in my life and see it as a doorway to a new opportunity, in this case to fulfil a destiny of working with my wife in starting a successful health food business.

* A former journal of The Christian Community.

Some of my happiest memories of Temple Lodge some twenty years ago are of working together with others to produce the string puppet plays (of *Tobit* and Goethe's *Green Snake and Beautiful Lily*). Evelyn's enthusiasm and anthroposophical knowledge made such ventures enjoyable and significant.

I also remember how much Evelyn exemplified the worldwide nature of our movement, with her extensive contacts and friends abroad. I was lucky enough to join Evelyn and Bert on one journey to visit the churches of East Germany. I remember serving whilst Evelyn celebrated (mostly in English) for these small dedicated congregations. (My extensive varied experience came in useful.) I cannot also forget how I missed my rendezvous in Cologne on the way back and spent three hours trying to find the Christian Community house. Evelyn was most concerned about my disappearance and cancelled the evening's lecture.

Irene Ellis
Stroud, Gloucestershire, England

My connection with Evelyn has mostly been during my several 'stays' in Temple Lodge, on and off during the 1960s onwards. Later I was out of the country for several years and I was only too happy to be able to stay in Temple Lodge when I wished to attend a conference and visit friends.

I found a very warm and welcoming atmosphere in Temple Lodge, and there would *always* be a number of very interesting people gathered around Evelyn at meal times, which guaranteed much stimulating conversation embracing the most varied subjects. Naturally I attended the Act of Consecration of Man whenever I was staying there and would learn much from her words of wisdom, which would accompany the service.

Evelyn was genuinely interested in the younger generation, and I think many young people felt very drawn to her. Without question, I would say that she has contributed *very much indeed* to the furtherance of both anthroposophy and The Christian Community.

Ivan Gibbons
London, England (Senior Lecturer in Cultural and Community Studies, Kensington and Chelsea College)

I worked with Evelyn Capel in establishing and running outreach adult education classes in Temple Lodge on behalf of the then Addison Adult Education Institute, which was one of the Inner London Education Authority's institutes and covered Hammersmith and Shepherds Bush. This was in 1979–80 and continued developments first initiated by Mrs Capel and my predecessor, Michael Newman.

We organised all sorts of classes in philosophy, comparative religion and history, and Mrs Capel made welcome to Temple Lodge many adult education students who otherwise would not even have known that the building existed.

Peter Heathfield
Hove, East Sussex, England

Through Evelyn Capel I came into The Christian Community. She has had an important influence on my life and, on a number of occasions when I was facing a crisis of one sort or another, her advice and counsel were immediately forthcoming and effective in helping me.

My first meeting with her came about through the advice of Sam Derry, whom I met at Rudolf Steiner House. At his suggestion I went to Glenilla Road church on Easter Sunday in 1951. This was an occasion on which the marionette show based on Goethe's fairy tale (*The Green Snake and the Beautiful Lily*) was presented. I was deeply impressed by all I experienced that day and it was the beginning of my connection with The Christian Community.

In January 1956, whilst I was a student at Hawkwood College, Evelyn Capel came to lecture and it was then that she and I became friends. Here it was, for the first time, that I experienced how objective her judgement could be on behalf of others, and I benefited from her counsel and intervention on my behalf.

She encouraged me to attend services at Benen House

and – later that same year – I became a member of The Christian Community.

In 1958, at Evelyn's suggestion, I went to the priests' seminar at Stuttgart. Although after a fairly short time in Stuttgart I realised that the priesthood was not the right vocation for me, I benefited in many directions from the year I spent there.

Between 1962 and 1964, whilst I was studying in London, I was able to live at Temple Lodge. During that time I became involved in the many activities that Evelyn initiated and came to see what qualities she had for organisation and for developing the life of the Community. I also began to read her books, which were a wonderful introduction to the theology of The Christian Community.

I began to see how effectively Evelyn was able to help members who became bereaved and experienced this personally when my own mother died.

Evelyn also had great expertise in helping friends in cases of a suicide. Here again I had personal experience of her concern and help when the son of a friend took his own life.

Having been connected with Temple Lodge since it was acquired for the West London Christian Community, I have seen how Evelyn's vision and energy have brought into being a wonderful centre for our work. This, I hope, will be a lasting memorial to her ministry.

Gillian Helfgott with Alissa Tanskaya

Bellington, New South Wales, Australia (extract from *Love you to Bits and Pieces*, published by Penguin Books Australia in 1996 – reproduced by kind permission). This is Gillian's story of her husband, the world-famous Australian pianist David Helfgott.

Friends had recommended [1986] that we stay at the Rudolf Steiner Lodge in Hammersmith, and their suggestion turned out to be ideal. The large Georgian house – the oldest residence in Hammersmith, tucked away between the Odeon Theatre and the overpass – had a surprisingly serene atmosphere. There was a beautiful rose garden, and flowerbeds glowed with summer blooms against a backdrop of shady trees. Upon our arrival, we were greeted by Dr Evelyn Keppel [Revd Evelyn Capel] and her husband Bert. David immediately felt at peace with the place and the people – which was just as well, because this was to be our base for the next five months.

There were two grand pianos for David to choose from: one in the dining room and one in the chapel, and David would often entertain the other Lodge guests at dinner time. Living at the Lodge was akin to living in a large family home, with groups of different relatives visiting all the time. The friendliness of the Steiner visitors, and their understanding of David, made for a very rewarding and happy time. Steiner teachers and people interested in Steiner's philosophy and educational methods came to the Lodge from all around the world, and we made many new friends during our stay.

Evelyn, a very efficient, clever, strong and determined woman, whom some people might have found challenging, had a great rapport with David. But while she was caring and kind to him, she would not let him get up to any of his tricks. He was, of course, completely dedicated to raiding the communal sugar and tea supplies, and Evelyn was quite firm about his naughtiness. On the other hand, she made him cups of tea and took him for outings in the garden, and I was grateful there was someone else to help contain his pranks.*

* Evelyn met David Helfgott again at a private reception following his concert at the Royal Albert Hall with the London Philharmonia Orchestra on 20 October 1997.

Margaret Gwyneth Lewis
London, England

When I lived in Richmond with a group of the New Atlantis Foundation, some of us started to study the works of Rudolf Steiner, and I began to visit Temple Lodge to hear lectures by Dr Ralph Twentyman and others. I also came to classes in projective geometry. I found these visits very stimulating.

Evelyn was wonderful in her support given to Katherine Barker, another member of the New Atlantis Foundation. Evelyn organised a memorial service for her, which I attended. I greatly admired the help she gave to the elderly, lonely and bewildered, as well as encouraging the young to widen their interests and continue their education.

I am sorry she has had to give up her work for others, but I am sure she will find the physical rest will give her more time to contemplate and fulfil her own spiritual needs.

Shireen Macniven
Cheltenham, Gloucestershire, England

I first met Evelyn Capel in May 1992 when I was looking for a place to stay in London while I began studying for a new career. At that time I didn't know anything about anthroposophy although I'd heard of Rudolf Steiner. I found Temple Lodge so beautiful but also homely and friendly that I immediately decided I'd like to stay. Mrs Capel came to meet me and surprised and delighted me by saying, 'You're very welcome to stay but if we decide we don't like you we'll ask you to leave!' Straight away I knew what kind of place it was.

I'd only been there about one week when my mother was taken seriously ill. For the next month we all went through a traumatic time and then she died. Mrs Capel was enormously supportive to me. Although I was not an 'anthropop', she counselled me and helped me through that time. Two more deaths in my close family followed in the next few months and I know I couldn't have coped without her calm acceptance of death and care for the living.

As I continued my new studies in holistic aromatherapy, Mrs Capel gave me great encouragement. I was shy and unsure of myself but she gave me confidence in myself and my abilities. She was interested that I lived in Cheltenham and used to talk to me about her time there when she was a young girl.

I used to visit Temple Lodge when I returned to London for further training and often Mrs Capel had just returned from a trip to Africa where she lived in mud huts with the villagers. Sometimes she would return late at night, having taken the tube or bus across London to visit a sick or dying friend or member of The Christian Community. I was full of admiration for an old lady who had such guts and determination and complete faith in God's protection of her. I was nervous of travelling alone at night in London.

Mrs Capel asked me to treat her once and invited me to work from Temple Lodge. I feel it is a privilege to know Mrs Capel and I find her an inspiring example of living one's life with intelligence and kindness. I feel sure that I was helped to find Temple Lodge to be there at that difficult time.

Patricia and Harold Mellor
Bury St Edmunds, Suffolk, England (Harold Mellor was one of the original trustees of the Benen Trust and its first secretary)

Evelyn had already given us sound advice on choosing a Rudolf Steiner school for our boys when in 1954 we joined one of her study groups in St John's Wood. Later these groups were held at Benen House in Draycott Place and we were able to attend there.

When Temple Lodge was to be purchased, Harold, who worked in the field of property in London, was asked to become a trustee of the newly formed Benen Trust, together with Mr Kitchin, Mrs McDougall and others. He undertook the secretary's duties. The Trust was established solely to purchase and look after Temple Lodge, and Evelyn was not a member of it.

Preparing the house entailed the forming of a nursery school (later the bookshop) and a chapel within the house in addition to the residential areas, and Patricia spent many hours painting walls and laying floor tiles.

Harold left the Trust after some years – long before the chapel was re-sited and other ventures were set up. Geographical moves and work changes brought about distancing, but in all these years one was always aware that Evelyn's steadfast spirit of leadership continued as strong as ever. We always missed our participation in her study groups where we learned so much and received guidance both practical and spiritual.

Then, in 1994, after previously meeting her at Gerald Bowen's funeral in Norwich, she came to visit us in Bury St Edmunds where we now live. She travelled by coach with remarkable stoicism, considering that she had not been well and was plagued with arthritis; and we were deeply touched by her generous determination to make contact again and to reassure us that our links with the past were not broken. She was a star in our lives.

Dr Michael Newman
Sydney, New South Wales, Australia (Senior Lecturer in Adult Education, University of Technology)

I met Mrs Capel in 1971 or thereabouts and was immediately intimidated. I was about thirty, a community education worker for the Inner London Education Authority, attached to Addison Adult Education Institute. I was also an atheist and eager to bring in some kind of revolutionary new dawn through the media of community democracy and community action. All my bravado dissipated on encounter with Mrs Capel. She was the minister for The Christian Community at Temple Lodge, and my job was to liaise with her in the management of a number of courses being run in conjunction with Addison at Temple Lodge.

While I only dimly knew what I was doing, Evelyn (I still have trouble using her first name) was utterly assured of what she was doing. While I claimed beliefs of a flower-powery political kind, she clearly had a spiritual and mystical vision that put me in awe. What is more, while I thought that the institute was using Temple Lodge, it became obvious that Mrs Capel was using me. With the utmost courtesy she would consult me about the courses to be run and then go ahead and organise what suited The Christian Community. I would attend to see to the enrolments, see to the payment of the speakers and at Mrs Capel's request (or was it gentle insistence?) chair the occasional session. Our relationship was constructed on the elegant pretence that I actually had some kind of influence over events.

Afterwards I wrote about these courses at Temple Lodge* and opined that none of my discomfort mattered because Mrs Capel had organised educational events that contributed a rarefied richness to the adult education programme of our part of London. Where else, for a purely nominal enrolment fee, could people gather in a beautiful Regency house and listen to a biodynamic farmer talk about how his cows positioned themselves to give meaning to a whole hillside? Where else could I and others listen to a leading London homoeopath talk of birds as *thoughts*? Where else could I listen to a person as remarkable as Mrs Capel herself expound Rudolf Steiner's educational ideas? I am no mystic. I came home to Australia and worked in the pragmatic world of trade unions for a number of years. I remain carefully sceptical about much of what was taught at Temple Lodge; but I readily acknowledge that in my encounters with Evelyn Capel and her toughness, her vision, her certainty, her courtesy, her dedication and, yes, when I had relaxed a little, her interest and friendship, I learnt something more about the difficult business of being human.

* Michael Newman *The Poor Cousin – A Study of Adult Education* (George Allen & Unwin, 1979).

Valerie Taylor
Aberdeen, Scotland

We came to Temple Lodge as a place to meet up with our friend Peter Heathfield, who played the piano for services there, although we lived in Forest Row where there was a Christian Community church.

We enjoyed the sense of community, the wonderful if sometimes eccentric elderly congregation, the warmth, the bees in the garden – a haven of elemental activity so close to Hammersmith roundabout. We enjoyed the sharing of each other. We always dressed in white for Whitsun, gathered and made posies of white flowers for everyone and my son shared out the white doves he had made.

My son was loved by the congregation. They understood each other wordlessly – from Janet [Evelyn's sister] at her special sandwich-preparing place in the kitchen, to Evelyn who would sit with Daniel, stroking Augusta together. One Whitsun Evelyn and Daniel both disappeared, having been deep in conversation. Later I glanced through the glass panel of the chapel and saw them – Evelyn giving Daniel a service which he had asked for. Silently I withdrew, not wishing to disturb a special moment.

I was aware of the gifts and challenges that Evelyn brought as a personality, yet we were always able to 'meet' her. Always in her sermons there was a phrase or sentence I needed to hear and could work with. The plays were always spontaneously good-humoured; we donned our clothes, read our parts and sang with no rehearsals.

In Evelyn's absences William Davie was always appreciated. One Ascension talk I particularly remember, and I appreciated his services.

There was life and goodness at Temple Lodge which transcended everything else. It was always there. Elsewhere I have been to worthy occasions yet something was lacking. At Temple Lodge one was able to embrace the humanity, gifts and frailties of people. This was no Essene community. We accepted each other for all our peculiarities, a goodness lived between us. Christ was present in those meetings. Temple Lodge was a community of Christians the like of which is rare in these times.

Ann Walsh
Wembley, Middlesex, England

After the war I worked in the Ruhr area of West Germany within a relief team of the Guide International Service in the sphere of rehabilitation. It was probably in 1948, when I was running camps for undernourished youths, that I felt the need of responsible German table graces to counter, for example, 'Wie die Adler aus den Lüften stürzen wir uns auf

Evelyn (left) with her sisters Edith and Janet at the steps of Temple Lodge, 1971.

An artist's sketch of Temple Lodge.

die Knifte!' [Like vultures from the sky, we pounce upon the fry.] Ken Walsh, who worked as the Control Commission Officer dealing with youth in Regierungsbezirk Arnsberg and with whom I shared a Christian Community background, suggested I ask 'Evelyn' Francis. I promptly wrote to *Mr* Evelyn Francis and by return received a pile of handwritten verses, 'some are by Dr Steiner, some are my own', and signed Evelyn Francis, ignoring the Mr! It was only later that I realised (not being English-born) that Evelyn is one of those names that can be given to either sex.

Having meanwhile married Ken Walsh and shared seven years with him in Germany, we settled in England after he was transferred to London. One day I received a desperate letter from a friend (Christian Community) in the Hague. An old friend of hers lived in London and was unsettled and in a bad state. She had gone through the war in Indonesia, had managed to stay out of the camps but her husband had been imprisoned by the Japanese and after the war there was a divorce. My friend had written to one of the priests but nothing had happened. So I took the matter up with Evelyn and had a long preliminary talk with her, giving her as much information as I could. She saw my friend's friend and was of much help to her.

One day, having been to the service at Temple Lodge, I had stayed on for the christening of the fourth little boy of a family. The father was blind and sang beautifully, unaccompanied. While the baptism was taking place, the three little brothers began to run around, round and through the pulpit, and Evelyn did not take a blind bit of notice. One of the little boys even came to stand next to her and held her hand. Nothing was interrupted and the new soul was duly received into 'the family'. Evelyn had very much her own way with such things. I can think of few, if any, priests who would be able to cope and continue so unperturbed!

Whereas in Holland, Germany and at Glenilla Road, I had never ventured into the service after Gospel reading and the sermon, I noticed with some dismay that at Temple Lodge there was no such discipline. People would happily come in at whatever time they arrived. But I was impressed when after a service Evelyn went over to a very-latecomer and said to her, 'I am so glad that you managed it!'

As time went by Evelyn became more and more the matron who did the rounds and did not like idleness. Many has been the time when little jobs were found for me between lunch and an afternoon session. Once they included proofreading. But it *did* give the feeling of belonging to a family where everyone was expected to do his or her bit.

I often quote Evelyn's tongue-in-cheek remark, that women are good enough to be saints but not priests! The local Church of England vicar to whom I had sent this comment, and who is for the ordination of women, put it in his monthly magazine, much to Evelyn's delight.

One aspect of the way Evelyn worked at Temple Lodge is perhaps not widely known but deserves to be. As Mrs Fisher, a longstanding [honorary] treasurer of that congregation, told me, Evelyn never drew a stipend. She followed what Rudolf Steiner had advocated: separating her work from any connection with money. This by no means implies that she went short – she did not. What was needed was provided, and she was thrifty almost to a fault on behalf of The Christian Community. It had always very much impressed Mrs Fisher that, whenever Evelyn received money after a talk or a visit, she would conscientiously hand it over. She was probably lucky in that she had some well-to-do members who were determined to look after her and from time to time apparently someone might take her out to buy her a new outfit. All this, of course, left her free to carry out any initiative irrespective of what it might entail financially. And it worked! She was very much her own woman.

Finally, from the days when she was training for management with Lyons, she herself told with great glee that she kept a little black book in which she pretended to write when the girls were misbehaving.

CHAPTER 4

A New Church

Alan Collins

Totnes, Devon, England (*see also* page 72)

The Act of Consecration of Man was the love of Evelyn's life. When she spoke she connected heaven and earth through her heart in a way that I will never forget. The inflections of her powerful voice offered ever new variations of its spiritual meanings. This was her special gift to the world. I found myself at Temple Lodge again and again.

Evelyn's dearest wish was to give this ritual a space worthy of it, where anyone could go and not be disturbed. I remember her joy as a local paper printed the story of planning permission being granted for a unique new chapel in Hammersmith! An extraordinarily large bequest had been given by a personal friend of Evelyn's, and other finances were also donated. It is a pity that money and differences of opinion have brought this dream to an end.* I hope that Evelyn will return one day to find her vision constructed!

In early 1995 Evelyn's ministry came to an abrupt end, through her own ill health. One day she beckoned me into the vault behind the kitchen and voiced her despair. I looked down at the model of the double-domed chapel, which had been taken from its pride of place in the entrance hall.

Then, to my surprise, she asked if I would take her to one of Benjamin Creme's talks. This gesture ended ten years of tension between the two of us, and a karmic knot was qui-

* Present plans are centred on modifying and improving the present chapel at Temple Lodge.

etly resolved. It remains a tribute to Evelyn that she could profoundly disagree with you and yet continue to love and cherish you. And, even if her words cut like a knife sometimes, her motives were the same as a surgeon's. She did what she thought was best for her 'patients', and the health of Temple Lodge was always uppermost in her mind.

'But where shall I go now?' Evelyn asked me on another occasion. It was then that I broke my own reserve. Putting my arm around her, I said that I would soon own a house with a granny annexe in Totnes where she could live if necessary. It was my turn to witness her facing a crisis, and it was my turn to comfort her. Yet Evelyn's stoicism was also, as always, in evidence. She had herself provided a home and work for many people with nowhere else to turn. I had spoken to many of them over the years and thought it a pity that they were not by her side now! That Sunday, sitting after lunch in the library with my memories, I wrote the following poem:

Christ in You
For Revd Evelyn Francis Capel
Easter 1995

When you have done enough to know
The nature of this changing world, and wisely
Played your unique part . . .
And found the pattern for each life below,
As if by accident, your wilful enterprise
Through every thought!

For with no thought of self you've found the way,
Without a care for self you've trod the path,
'Til darkness fell . . .
And 'though those fools may praise you every day,
Just as they've heaped the blame and had a laugh,
You'll never tell!

But standing on a hallowed spot alone,
With mind determined on a dual purity,
You'll make your vow . . .

And when the consequence of every act is known,
And when the bloody battle almost lost to Thee,
He'll help somehow!

When all your words and worldly wishes flee,
And each earthly desire has been and gone,
Their clouds depart . . .
Then out of emptiness will shine on thee,
God's light, as on His Son
And fill thy heart!

Then on that hill where doubt comes to an end,
In that bright inner blaze of light and bliss,
God will be known . . .
And, even though a darker test He'll send,
There is no greater height and no more words than this:
'My Lord, Thy Will be done!'

John Hugo
Cilycwm, Carmarthenshire, Wales

In the course of a conversation on the subject of reincarnation, I asked Evelyn in what sphere of activity she would wish to find herself in a further life on Earth. With a twinkle in her eye she answered, 'As a builder.' This all-encompassing response characterised her entire approach to her priestly undertakings. To build has been her *raison d'être*: initially to create centres providing the physical basis for pastoral and cultural activity, and within those centres to develop and disseminate the corpus of knowledge and experience of Christian life acquired through her profound understanding of anthroposophy.

Her independent spirit found her in earlier days in a pioneering environment as typified by her christening of our youngest child in a 'chapel' contrived in a little room behind a baker's shop in North London. Such expediencies were soon surmounted and firm foundations were laid down in succeeding stages, as we were to experience at Sloane Square [Benen House] and Temple Lodge. Both bore the stamp of Evelyn's personality. In the early days at the Lodge she made a comment that one might imaginatively construe as a reflection of building propensities millennia ago. 'What we really need is a sphinx on either side of the entrance.' Would it be mischievous to envisage a participation in the spiritual impulses that gave rise to the vast constructions undertaken in Egypto-Chaldean times!

What of the future? 'The future is in Wales,' she said and, although her constitution was being increasingly taxed, she journeyed repeatedly from London to Lampeter to bring the Act of Consecration to an embryo congregation. It was her great hope and intention to make fruitful connections with the University of Wales in Lampeter in order to bring an awareness of anthroposophy into the life of the college. Sadly her declining health did not permit her to achieve this aim. Nevertheless, the bringing of the Act of Consecration into that part of Wales comprised a spiritual deed implanting a seed for the future.

Contemplating the distant future, we can be assured that the individuality that we have come to love and respect, in

Evelyn and her sisters Winifred (far left) and Edith (centre) on an outing in Scotland.

whatever sphere of human activity it will be found, will continue a process of building: building in freedom a pathway to the Christ, the Helper and Guide.

Stuart Page
Tunbridge Wells, Kent (architect to the former New Church Project at Temple Lodge)

At intervals throughout my studies and subsequent professional career, I have had contact with anthroposophy but not the commitment and dedication I have seen and experienced in others. Barbara Manteuffel, the architect selected by Evelyn Capel for the new church project at Temple Lodge, was an exceptional person with great understanding and feeling for materials, building form and, most importantly, for the people within and without the architecture. I had worked with Barbara in her studio at Parrock Wood and, when I established a practice in Tunbridge Wells, she in turn came to help us. During these visits we discussed projects and the difficulties of realising quality in buildings; from conception to completion the path is frustrating and indirect. The need for a successful building to be three works of art was never far from our minds: the client-architect relationship, the architect-builder relationship, and the building itself.

When Barbara died on 5 October 1989, she had been working with Evelyn on the design of the new church for just over one year. Her work was interrupted at a stage when the overall form and siting of the building were decided but the detail needed resolution. The invitation from The Christian Community (London West) to develop the design was welcome but came as a surprise, because there are many architects with wider experience and involvement in anthroposophy. However my meeting with the trustees and with Evelyn went well; I was appointed to develop the project and take it forward to planning approval and, if funds were available, to assist in its realisation.

Evelyn understood the importance of Barbara's design and showed a rare determination, for a client, to pursue the concept. I was not involved until long after the inception of the building, but it was clear that Evelyn and Barbara had shared a knowledge of how the church would respond to the needs of Temple Lodge and, in turn, to the wider needs of The Christian Community. Sections had been drawn through the building, outline elevations had been prepared, and each was noted with brief messages, memoranda and notes as reminders of details yet to be resolved. By the time the last of these notes were being added, Barbara may have known that someone else would have to share these details and that the resolution of her concepts and the structural response to the sacraments would be in the hands of another architect.

Working with and restoring Barbara's model of the church was an extraordinary experience: the forms had been created internally and externally in modelling clay and I felt both the architect's presence and the completed building. Presenting the model and the drawings to the Community, and their acceptance, was a project milestone and an achievement for the concept. Evelyn showed great understanding of how much could be achieved: the building should be started to provide impetus for fund-raising but might not be completed for many years. We discussed the interior, and she felt it was something for the future, that others might contribute to the completion of the inner forms and finishes. But there was always the quiet, understated determination to move forwards.

Participating in this work has been a rare and intense experience. Barbara's legacy to me has been the sharing of an insight into a new and complex architecture. I have no doubt that this is the result of her response to Evelyn's vision as a client.

Fiona Tweedale
Coleg Elidyr, Rhandirmwyn, Carmarthenshire, Wales

I first met Evelyn Francis – as she then was – in the early 1940s, with the Second World War raging all around us. I thought at the time: this one will be quite a character in the circle of priests! And that has been proved true over a span of more than fifty years of her ministry. Things always happened wherever she was: first in Glenilla Road, the Christian Community house in North London, later in Benen House, Chelsea, and much later at Temple Lodge, Hammersmith. She worked tirelessly with congregations, study groups, lectures, conferences, counselling, to mention just a few.

In later years, she and her husband, Bert, held a great ideal before them – to build a church in the grounds of the beautiful garden of Temple Lodge (where the artist Frank Brangwyn had lived for many years). Plans were actually drawn up by Barbara Manteuffel for a truly beautiful and living building in which would be experienced by all who saw it a progression through Goethean metamorphosis from the entrance, through the congregation area to the sanctuary and the altar where the sacraments of The Christian Community would be celebrated. In a publicity handout at the time, Stuart Page, the architect who continued the work after Barbara's untimely death, described her brief as follows:

The Sacraments of The Christian Community have a structure of their own. It is the Lemniscate, or figure of eight. The upper circle belongs to the Spiritual World, the lower circle the World of people on Earth. At the crossing point between the two, the risen Christ stands. The Archangel Michael is His countenance, and His celebrating priest from the Earthly point of view, and is seen standing with them at this point. Everything that supports the action of a Sacrament should become part of this fundamental structure. It should form the starting point of the architecture of the church building.

A large fund for this building had meanwhile been established.

On one of my visits to Temple Lodge on a beautiful summer day in the 1980s, I walked round the garden with Bert and Evelyn as they described with joy and enthusiasm just how and where the new church would be. One was fired with joy at the prospect.

Because of this ideal being carried in hearts and minds for many years, I venture here to include an outline of this plan especially for the many visitors to Temple Lodge who came to know and love it dearly. The drawings show how worthy and beautiful it would be. Evelyn's comment at the time was:

The Sacraments are the inspiration for the Christianity within our hearts. They form a way of living and working in modern times that allows people a Christian vision of what it is to be human. For this new Christian understanding, a new type of architecture is required. Although we are grateful for the architectural beauties from the past, it remains that the old Christian architecture no longer speaks to our modern times.

In the end, destiny has taken a hand in the breakdown of Evelyn's health, which has meant the building plans are on hold for the time being – but the ideal is nevertheless a seed for the future and, if it is the will of the spiritual world, it will take place when the time is ripe. Meanwhile let us take the images of the church-to-be into our hearts and souls. Rudolf Steiner spoke much on the importance of 'living architecture' and the healing effects it has on all those who see it. Last year [1996], when Evelyn came to stay in Wales, I spoke to her on these lines and a gleam came into her eyes and she said, 'Yes! It is certainly true and beautiful.'

Evelyn's achievements throughout her life are a living testimony of her soul forces, completely devoted to the Christ and the sacraments of The Christian Community.

Thank you, Evelyn! May these years of your achievements and victories through problems live on in you in shining memory. The ideals we walk towards will fill us all with courage, and the Michaelic forces may take them up into the new millennium for the etheric Christ and the consciousness soul. Bless you and thank you, Evelyn!

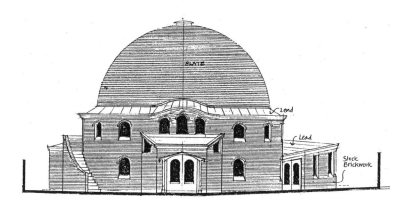

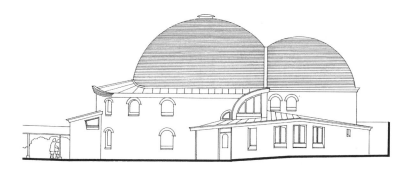

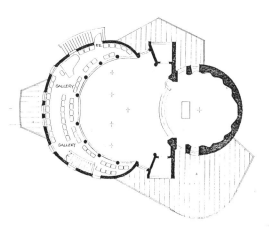

Stuart Page's revised plans of Barbara Manteuffel's design for a new church.

CHAPTER 5

Help and Guidance

Barbara Adcock
Chichester, West Sussex, England

I will try to put a few thoughts on paper but I fear they will be very inadequate to express my admiration and gratitude to Evelyn Capel for her invaluable practical advice and help to me and my family. All-important, of course, has been her priestly work, which has changed our lives by giving us encouragement and inspiration in our spiritual struggles.

My first meeting with Evelyn was in 1942 in Mrs Roger-Smith's house in Capel, Surrey. She gave the small group a short talk on the Sermon on the Mount. The impact was so powerful that it led me into The Christian Community where I have remained ever since. Our family home was never near enough for us to be in Evelyn's congregation, but she took the trouble to visit us in the country, giving me wise advice on the upbringing of my two sons and one daughter. One of her many gifts was a habit of turning up when most needed, when we had reached a crossroad or some crisis. When I mentioned this to her she said simply, 'That comes through the Work.'

Before I discovered the Community, my elder son was baptised in the Anglican Church and, of course, relations expected the same for the next children. Evelyn came to see me, swept all fears aside and arranged a baptism for my baby daughter and second son – three years old, but still unbaptised because of wartime conditions. (This delay may have had some significance in his destiny, as in 1971 he was ordained a priest in The Christian Community.) So in January 1946 Evelyn conducted the service in The Studio,* a chapel of those early days, and it was the first Christian Community baptism my family, a few friends, relations and I had attended. We found it strange, but I know people were moved by the beauty of all that took place. In her wisdom Evelyn had asked Stanley Drake to be godfather to my son, which was always a great blessing for him.

The next crisis was education. My elder son, ten years old and highly strung, was considered backward in reading, although able in maths, by his preparatory school. He was kept in a lower class than his friends and was unhappy. Evelyn turned up saying, 'The eleven-plus is looming, which can do great harm. Parents worry. Children become anxious. Avoid it at all costs. You must move house and send them all to Michael Hall.' This was just what I had wanted for them but Evelyn gave me the necessary impetus. My husband, not enamoured of his public school education, agreed to make the sacrifice of a longer train journey to work. In two months we were settled near Forest Row. Thus followed schooldays happy and enriching for the three of them and for me as well because I was able to hear lectures, join in a German class and attend a study group for parents under Captain Field.

During those years I was in the Forest Row congregation, later in the Kings Langley congregation. Evelyn came occasionally to give a talk which I, like many others, tried never to miss. I read most of her books as they were published and a great many articles in The Christian Community journals. These were a constant inspiration and guide. Evelyn's great gifts in her clear thinking and writing have given us a light to enter more fully into the sacraments and to understand hidden knowledge in the Bible, like *The Timeless Storyteller* on the parables. Her tireless study of anthroposophy has enabled her to give it to us in an understandable form. We are deeply grateful for this.

Evelyn's influence has been far-reaching, in several European countries as well as in Germany. Her pioneering work

* Maitland Park Villas, London NW3.

in South Africa (my country) has been invaluable. Affection and admiration have grown steadily for her through the years.

I think we all know that Evelyn is a superb counsellor. She spent two days with my niece and most certainly saved her from a nervous breakdown in 1964. She was restored by Evelyn's compassion, deep spiritual knowledge and bracing practical approach. Since his baptism my son has had the benefit of Evelyn's faithful friendship and invaluable advice. She has never failed him.

May I join everyone else in saying 'Thank you, dear Evelyn,' and in wishing you a happy retirement.

David Andriesse
Ruislip, Middlesex, England

I met Revd Capel only once, in May 1987, but the occasion was of wide spiritual significance, not known to me at the time.

It was only last year that I read Richard Leviton's *The Imagination of Pentecost*. There he records the fact of an explosion of spiritual visionary experiences by individuals worldwide in 1987. I had not known about this, but my own experiences during a few years centred on 1987 confirmed that a veil was indeed thrown back at that time and that Christ-based spiritual communications came thick and fast.

I do not think it a coincidence that I was motivated in 1987 to ring up and ask for an opportunity to talk to Evelyn Capel because I had known for thirty years previously about her spiritual work and leadership of The Christian Community.

Julian Armstrong
Milton Keynes, Buckinghamshire, England (Julian is from Camphill Milton Keynes Communities for Adults with Learning Difficulties and these words have been written down from a conversation with Morwenna)

Evelyn christened Julian, whose mother, Marjory, was very supportive of The Christian Community. Julian joined Camphill Milton Keynes Community as an adult companion. When visiting his mother in London, they both attended the service and, when Marjory Armstrong died, Evelyn took the service. After that she often invited Julian to London and for lunch after the service. In the afternoon, they went out to the theatre, sometimes accompanied by Julian's friend Mandy. Once they went on a boat trip on the Thames. Quite often Evelyn travelled to Delrow to see Julian take part in plays and she also came to see him in a play in Milton Keynes. Julian was invited to Evelyn's retirement party before she moved to the country.

Julian loves her dearly and says that she loves him.

Revd Allan Bell
London, England

I am a priest in holy orders of the Church of England and met Evelyn Capel in my first year of training to the priesthood, about twelve years ago.

We met only the once, but the meeting had a profound effect on my life. At the time I was struggling with the narrow definitions of priesthood in the Anglican Communion and had almost given up my training when I met Evelyn. What struck me about her was her essence of priesthood.

We talked about many things that afternoon, and I left her with the strong sense that it was all right to be different as a priest and to be unconventional.

Despite many doubts and reservations I was ordained a priest two years ago and have stuck to Evelyn's advice, despite pressure to conform, to be the kind of priest that I believe that God is calling me to be in His world. I am eternally grateful for her encouragement and support.

Isla Bourke
London, England

I met Evelyn Capel after a brush with cancer in 1986 and a determination to extend the boundaries of orthodox medicine as far as my own illness was concerned. Having found the people at Steiner House somewhat introspective, I made my way to Hammersmith and found Evelyn with one foot in the outside world – literally. In a stylish hat she was sweeping the snow from the front doorstep of Temple Lodge. She invited me into her study at once and, when her dear cat, Augusta, jumped on my lap, commented that it was probably my coat that was the attraction!

I recall little of our conversation but felt that Temple Lodge had been placed at my disposal. I sat for hours over untidy piles of magazines in the (then) modest vegetarian restaurant, learning about organic garden systems and the 'whole person' approach to illness. I browsed in the well-stocked bookshop. Then in the spring and summer along came Audrey Bayfield, with the annual painting classes encouraged by Evelyn. Handling prisms, I was a child again, entranced by the healing effects of colour and by expeditions to paint in the open air. There were other excursions and talks, which helped me cope with my illness, and the healing touch of Evelyn during the Act of Consecration of Man.

I became something of a Temple Lodge 'groupie' for a year or so, but Evelyn never encouraged dependency and I soon went on my way feeling strengthened and renewed. As I grew to know Evelyn better, I marvelled at everything she appeared to have achieved in service to mankind. A recent history of Somerville (the Oxford women's college, which Evelyn attended) describes its pioneering energy and the fact that its students, from an early stage, acquired the reputation of being 'difficult'. Evelyn may have been 'difficult' but she could also inspire intense loyalty. I noticed that the honorary treasurer Cecelia Fisher – now ninety-five – was still making an arduous daily journey to Temple Lodge at the age of eighty-five!

Evelyn loved people, members of her movements or not. I am told she liked to start and/or finish her workshop sessions with a few lines by Rudolf Steiner: 'The sun gives light to the plants, for the sun loves the plants. So one man gives soul-light to others when he loves them.' Evelyn truly loved those she helped. May we continue to take this love into the world on her behalf.

As a voluntary temporary carer for Evelyn during the winter of 1995/96, I was aware that she was finding it very difficult to move on and that her good deeds had become overshadowed by the problems of her advancing years; she was by then eighty-four. As I tap thousands of words into my computer to complete this book, I know that the balance has now been redressed. We love you, Evelyn. You have been a shining example of public service all over the world.

The Earl Pat Castle Stewart
Babcary, Somerset, England (company secretary, The Christian Community Trustees Ltd)

Evelyn Capel has played a part in various aspects of developments in my life. In 1952 she suggested that I and my fiancée at that time go to Hereford to meet a Mr Dorrell who was manager of the Co-op Farms. My fiancée and I were looking for a post in which I would be farm pupil or apprentice in order to learn my trade. This journey to Hereford was important since, although I did not end up working for Mr Dorrell, I did find on that journey the place where my fiancée and I were able to settle and marry, and I served an apprenticeship there for two and a half years. This could perhaps have been described as having been a precarious life situation at the time, and it certainly broke a situation in which I didn't know which way to move!

I have read Evelyn's books and have found them very helpful and fairly definitive with regard to what the sacraments are all about. This was particularly important in that I read about Sacramental Consultation when I was quite young (about twenty). This was of particular importance for me in getting through what was a very mixed up and difficult period, although it was not with Evelyn that I entered into this particular sacrament. It has been a great surprise to me to find out how many members and friends of The Christian Community don't even know that this particular sacrament exists, and it's quite possible I would not have known if I had not read about it in Evelyn's books.

Evelyn was a clear and forceful speaker and saw the need

to reach out to new areas of experience. Temple Lodge Publishing has produced a great number of books which it has been very important to have published and in circulation.

Hers was certainly a life of extraordinary and sustained effort over so many decades.

Alan Collins
Totnes, Devon, England (*see also* page 57)

I had been sent insane in 1974 when I was thirty years old by an experience that followed nine years of exhaustive philosophical enquiry. Since then I had lived on a razor's edge, never knowing from one day to the next if I would wake up with 'soul aflame and heart afire' – battling to control a cauldron of emotional force and mental energy.

One day in 1979 I awoke in that (psychotic) condition again. I remember conversing with a voice, yet knowing that this conversation was nothing but an unconscious conflict bubbling to the surface. On that occasion I turned up asking for help at the Rudolf Steiner bookshop in Museum Street, where a gentlewoman got Evelyn Capel on the phone who simply gave me directions from there.

Opening the door of Temple Lodge, Evelyn showed me to a seat in her study, under a picture of the Christ. She left me alone for a moment before returning with a chair to sit beside me, and began to speak of my exceptional courage. This was most unexpected! I knew her to have some degree of clairvoyance, as what she said then carried the same import as a life preview given to me in 1975 by another. After many negative experiences (of four years of psychiatric treatment) my faith and confidence was thus restored. Once more I was comforted under this 'raincloud of knowable things' and by finding someone else who saw in me much more than this chameleon self!

That day she knew that my condition had to burn itself out, and I needed (lithium) salt and another stay in St Bernard's asylum. She said only that which was enough, which remained our secret and our bond. I expected to be barred from seeing her again, as is the general rule, but battling with inertia and depression I dragged myself to Temple Lodge on Thursdays and Sundays from that day on. I had a timetable of a kind, so I had places to go, which kept me from my solitude and bed, which are as death to anyone in depression, as many of you will know.

I observed how she protected me from too much scrutiny, when I was feeling vulnerable or could not answer personal questions, by what might have seemed rude interruptions. On Sundays, during the short weekly address, her telepathic sensitivity gave her other opportunities to add something to those secret words that she had spoken that day but of which only she and I could grasp the import. Other manic/Luciferic episodes followed, along with their Ahrimanic aftermaths, until I returned from India in 1986 after an invitation from Sai Baba.

This seven-year period (after the preceding darkest phase of my life) seemed interminable and my illness incurable, but Evelyn's stoic attitude and constant faith in my recovery – from one so clearly grounded in reality – helped me not to lose my own faith. She officiated at my marriage and the baptisms of my two children, which were both added compensations to help me through this awful trial.

Evelyn stood as a way through which God gave me the experience to deal with an esoteric fact that cannot lawfully be communicated to one who has not found such things out. As the saying goes, 'Those who know do not say; those who say do not know.' Evelyn knew, and she helped me come to terms with it; and all these years she never said a word about it to anyone! In service to their kind, to such as Evelyn can the secrets be revealed.

John Dorrell
Pershore, Worcestershire, England

It is impossible to exaggerate the value of Evelyn's friendship and guidance lasting throughout a lifetime.

My late wife, Grace, was an anthroposophist from birth, all the time searching diligently. Meeting Evelyn during 1943 brought a flowering that was to enrich and enlighten our lives for over fifty years. We occasionally used our home for her services and lectures. I remember particularly a series on William Blake, as well as others, all paving an illuminating path to anthroposophy.

Her monthly newsletter, *Companions of the Inner Life*, provided a lifeline to those of us unable to attend in London. Her books too, of course, all helped us to find our way into Rudolf Steiner's work.

Without doubt the most personal effect of Evelyn's influence was to arrange for our daughter Deborah to come to us for adoption at her birth in April 1945.

During 1976 I developed a throat cancer. Evelyn introduced me to Dr Twentyman and the Cancer Research Institute in Arlesheim. The continued daily use of Iscador and other remedies reminds me each day of her blessing!

You will see how the presence of Evelyn has permeated every facet of our lives, and so of others who will follow us.

I had the last opportunity to meet Evelyn when she was staying with the two ladies in Wales [1996], and I was happy to see her so very well attended among friends.

Renate Edmonds
Tavistock, Devon, England

Evelyn Capel has greatly influenced my outlook on life and way of thinking.

I first met Evelyn at a private memorial service held for the late Dr John Raeside, who was one of a number of homoeopathic doctors so tragically killed in that fateful plane crash at Staines in June 1972. This first impression of someone who did not dread death nor wallow in emotional sympathy for others, but had real ideas and convictions about life after death and the possibility of reincarnation, has stayed with me ever since.

Evelyn did not only awaken my spiritual curiosity but has also tended this early seed. She was especially helpful while my late husband lay suffering from cancer and was to be found at his hospice bedside every day for the last two weeks or so of his life. She supported me in my faith and helped him die, her husband Bert faithfully chauffeuring her daily from Hammersmith to Sydenham!

Evelyn has seen my family grow up. She has christened my children: Thomas, Daniel and Kate, and brought them to confirmation. She was always understanding, never critical, even when my son Thomas appeared with torn jeans at his sister's confirmation ceremony! When I remarried in October 1987, she was an integral part of our blessing ceremony. I would call her my spiritual mentor, and I am greatly indebted to her for making me aware of my spiritual ego and the spiritual dimension of life.

I feel very privileged to have known her and want to take this opportunity to thank her for all her support and friendship over the years. My husband, Mike, and I wish her a pleasant 'Lebensabend', which she so rightly deserves.

Lisa Filon
Selsdon, Surrey, England

My family (husband, daughter, sisters-in-law and I) went to many of Mrs Capel's most interesting lectures and also to services at Temple Lodge.

Our life was somewhat changed and our thoughts much influenced by Mrs Capel. She led us to greater depth of spirituality and more understanding of Rudolf Steiner.

Lily Forge
Hindhead, Surrey, England

Evelyn has helped me so much, but you need to know my background before you can understand how much she means to me.

I came to England in 1939, as a Jewish refugee, with my mother, sister and brother. We stayed with relatives and friends for three years; then my mother and brother went to London to find work and my sister and I went to Camphill, near Aberdeen. (I have been told that we both had meningitis as small children.)

We stayed at various Camphill centres and finally settled at Botton, where my sister still lives. By that time I had met

Evelyn at a conference in Keswick. In 1967 I met John, who came to us from Delrow, and straight away we fell in love, but John was sent away and we were separated. When Evelyn heard about this, she encouraged us both to make an independent life outside Camphill. She said I was an intelligent lady and that being behind the four walls of Camphill was nonsense!

Revd Peter Allen married us in October 1979, when John was seventy-one and I was fifty. In spite of others trying to persuade us to go back to Camphill, we went and lived in hotels, then a flat, in Surrey. John looked after me like father and mother put together, and I am so grateful to him. From then on Evelyn invited us both to Temple Lodge on many occasions and made us most welcome. I am very grateful to her for having confidence in us both; she gave us a new lease of life.

Sadly John and I were married for only eight years before he died from a stroke; then Evelyn, who was very caring, told me I was in her charge whenever I was staying at Temple Lodge. She befriended me, made sure I mixed with all the guests, and took me up to the restaurant if she found me alone. I joined in the various activities that Evelyn arranged, including painting. I helped her dry dishes in the kitchen and became even more friendly with her. And she gave me jobs to do, such as distributing cards at Easter, Christmas, and other festivals. She cried on my shoulder when her husband, Bert, died; so, as I grew stronger, I was able to support her as well.

My visits to Temple Lodge (and other Christian Community centres) have always been very spiritual. With Evelyn, the Act of Consecration of Man, which has a great deal in it, helped and encouraged me in many ways. I didn't know how to express myself and this spiritual service was the answer. I want Evelyn to know that it has been very uplifting. Evelyn performed my husband John's funeral service, where she sprinkled water on the coffin. This was a great comfort, and I would like to have a Christian Community funeral myself.

Evelyn always used to say to me, 'Christmas and Easter at Temple Lodge wouldn't be the same without you.' Now Rachael Shepherd (the new priest) says the same thing, so I continue to enjoy my visits there. They still give me a new lease of life.

Virginia Gilmer
London, England

Evelyn Capel helped me at the time my cat was lost, three days before I had to leave for a stay of a number of months in Australia. My cat had escaped from a bathroom window of people in Kings Langley who had agreed to take care of her while I was away. Telling Evelyn of my plight – she herself was a great cat lover and had a cat of her own for many years – Evelyn told me not to worry and that the animal kingdom and hierarchies looked after each animal in a special way. She then produced a special prayer for the animals, which she advised me to read.

The next day I went from London to Kings Langley to search a last time for my cat. Lo and behold I found her in a neighbour's shack under a pile of wood and took her back to London to be looked after by the person who was to stay in my flat while I was away.

Mrs Capel's kind words and help in this matter helped to ease my mind and quell a lot of the anxiety that had arisen during this time.

Dorothy Goodman
Sanderstead, Surrey, England

I first met Evelyn in 1953 at the Goetheanum, during a summer 'English' week. It was a very brief encounter, but in a significant place, and I believe that she remembered it when I had occasion to consult her five years later. This concerned an unusual and problematic human relationship, which turned out to be a lifelong and important one for me. Later I spoke to Evelyn about some of my own 'inner' difficulties.

After The Christian Community [London West] moved to Hammersmith I did not often go there, but when my mother died in 1993 I sought Evelyn's advice on what was best to read, etc, and was very grateful for her help. I have found her book *Death: The End is the Beginning* especially valuable around the times when loved ones have died.

I have very much appreciated Evelyn's clarity of thought and perception. I picture how she would sit quietly listening and hearing what one wanted to say even if it were not well expressed. Her response was always relevant and measured, combining sympathy with honesty. True to her work with *The Philosophy of Spiritual Activity*, she respected and encouraged one's individual freedom and initiative, carefully offering them a helping hand.

From our conversations I always took with me a mood of positivity and serenity, which is good to recall!

Alfred Dowuona Hammond
London, England

I have known Mrs Capel since 1971. I first met her at Glenilla Road Christian Community. It was at Easter time, and there was a lecture/conference in which she spoke, describing how Africans receive their guests in a way and manner that, as an African, I did not know of. This appealed to me so much that after the lecture I enquired about her and learned that she had travelled to South Africa and Rhodesia as a priest and a teacher.

Later on I discussed the lecture with Lennart, the then housekeeper at Steiner House, who told me that she held psychology classes at Temple Lodge.

I came to know The Christian Community through the late Cecil Harwood when I went to Steiner House to enquire about Rudolf Steiner and his *Study of Man*. During our conversation he realised that I was a Christian and recommended that I join The Christian Community. So he arranged for me to go to Glenilla Road to meet Irene Taylor, then one of the priests there. Later on, after the 1971 Easter lecture and Irene's move to Scotland, I changed to Temple Lodge Christian Community.

At Temple Lodge I was soon invited to become a server. I

Evelyn with Alfred Dowuona Hammond, 1979 (photo: Juliet van Otteren).

started serving as a left server and Mrs Capel then recommended that I try to do right-hand as well. I served both sides so well that I became a server for all occasions, such as weddings, christenings, etc.

Then there came an invitation from a Nigerian pastor, inviting a branch of The Christian Community to be inaugurated there. Mrs Capel discussed this with me, and I suggested that first of all the person ought to be invited here to be trained as a priest, or leaflets sent to him before that invitation should be pursued.

So we agreed that it would be appropriate to write and publish a book and then send a copy to the enquirer. This brought about the writing of our *Christ in the Old and New Testaments*.

Mrs Capel has been my spiritual mentor because I always consult her about whatever I find difficult to understand and to do. To awaken my potential in this way, she recommended *Metamorphosis of the Soul* by Rudolf Steiner. She has been a great person in my life who has taught me how to look at life from both the inward and outward aspects. And it has been a great reward to me indeed.

Mrs Capel has written a lot of books, but for me *The Tenth Hierarchy* is the one that appeals most.

She has a love for Africa and Africans. She has travelled to Rhodesia, South Africa and Ghana and has made a lot of African friends. I remember when we travelled to Ghana on separate trips and I traced her to where she had lodged and invited her to tour the old town of Accra, called Jamestown.

Mrs Capel to me has a very simple approach to life in the way she handles things, and especially when she is conducting the services. She makes sure that everybody receives the Communion even though at times the congregation becomes more than the bread prepared; she manages to get everyone to have the Communion. And also, when we are doing plays at Temple Lodge, she tries to fit everybody into the play.

To me she has a very wonderful approach to every person and has a very lovable personality.

Edna Jones
Hockley, Essex, England

My friendship with Revd Capel began forty years ago. My son was then fifteen and he used to be a server at Temple Lodge. Evelyn knew my daughter and my sister as well, and my eldest grandson was baptised by Evelyn.

There are so many people who have been helped by Evelyn, including me. She was always there for me. I could tell Evelyn things that I couldn't tell anybody else. I could tell her everything I was thinking. I could bare my soul to her but to no one else. She gave me insight and enabled me to stand outside myself and see things as they really were.

Evelyn often gave me guidance as to *why* things were happening and what was required of me to deal with them. She showed me the way but then left *me* to cope with life and make the decisions. You knew in your heart that she was right. And she gave me the confidence to do what each particular situation required.

I was never bored in Evelyn's lectures. She held your attention. She spoke to *everyone* in the room. You just listened and your mind didn't wander. She made you see things in a more enlightened way. She had such a great understanding of everything.

After our first meeting, it was Temple Lodge and Evelyn for the rest of my life. I even met her in town for tea and talk. It is difficult to put into words, but she was just *there* for every occasion. I feel very privileged to have known Revd Evelyn Capel.

Julian Koenig
Oxford, England

I have known Evelyn Capel since about 1974, and she did a lot to help my mother and myself when we were in some difficulty in life, and I have been (since 1980) a member of The Christian Community, through her influence, and continue to support it.

The fact that Evelyn was able to run an organised programme of activities at Temple Lodge in the seventies and eighties was enormously important to me when I was living in London. She helped me find a spiritual perspective on life at a time when I was recovering from a nervous breakdown and was overwhelmed by the problem of death and attempted to kill myself with petrol in 1979 after the death of my mother's sister from cancer in 1975. She visited me in hospital and gave me things to do, such as reviewing her book on Christian meditation for *The Threshing Floor** and attending a conference on reincarnation on Iona in 1981 when I was recovering.

I visited her in Wales in July last year and at the Raphael Centre in December and February [1997]; I am full of gratitude to her for all that she has done for us.

* A former journal of The Christian Community.

John Lees
London, England (former trustee of The Christian Community/London West and former manager of Temple Lodge Press)

I had the privilege of working closely with Evelyn at Temple Lodge for three years from 1987 to 1990, during the years immediately following the death of Bert Capel. She had a reputation for being a 'difficult' person. And certainly, during the time that I worked at Temple Lodge, there were rows, disagreements and upsets with various people. However, these matters paled into insignificance in comparison with the many unique qualities that Evelyn possessed – her intelligence, her vision, her devotion and loyalty to The Christian Community (in spite of her concerns about its lack of vision and courage), her indomitable willpower, her accessibility and availability, her ease in communicating with learned pastors about 'high theology', whilst retaining 'the common touch' when necessary, and so on. But one thing, above all else, characterised, for me, Evelyn's genius: namely, her relationship with death. Walking with Evelyn in the 'shadow of death' was an unforgettable experience. And, fortunately for me, I had the privilege of doing so on two occasions – in 1988 and 1989.

In 1988 the mother of my partner visited this country. She lived in Eastern Europe, was an anthroposophist and spent about three months in Switzerland and Britain each year. And it was on these occasions, over a period of seven years, that I had got to know her. When she arrived in the country, she was already unwell but reasonably mobile and perfectly clear of mind. But she spent most of the time in my flat in London and didn't go out very much. One day, as she was in the kitchen washing the pots, she said that she was feeling a bit odd and that she was concerned because her skin had turned yellow. I contacted my general practitioner, who made a home visit, promptly arranged for her to be admitted to the local hospital and said that he thought she had cancer of the liver. She died in hospital about ten days later.

Evelyn met my 'mother-in-law' for the first time on her deathbed. It was about four days before she died and Evelyn performed the sacrament of Anointing. As I recall, Evelyn was somewhat excited after meeting 'this lovely woman'. And this seemed to me to be an entirely appropriate response, since it was, indeed, a remarkable and memorable occasion. I remember collecting Evelyn from Temple Lodge and driving along Westway towards the hospital on a rather blustery and wet Sunday evening as the dark clouds rolled across the sky. I also remember the service itself – reading the Lord's Prayer in English and Polish, and afterwards joking about the Catholic priest whom my 'mother-in-law' had humoured earlier that day when he performed the last rites. And, finally, I remember the feelings of joy, peacefulness and serenity, and the beauty and matter-of-factness of the occasion, which had taken place without any trace of sentimentality. My 'mother-in-law' was indeed a happy person that evening. She had lived a long, active and fulfilled life and was ready for death. She was looking forward to meeting her long-deceased friends and loved ones in the life after death.

I visited her on my own two or three times after that, but these visits were quite different. For the most part the mood had changed radically and bore no resemblance to the mood of the Anointing. Warmth had been replaced by cold, fullness by emptiness, contentment and joy by unease and fear. Indeed, one visit was positively chilling and frightening. My 'mother-in-law' was speaking, but her voice was unreal and distant – as though she was speaking from some space or chasm deep down inside her. I remember feeling 'my hair stand on end'.

When I took 'counsel' with Evelyn about these events and contrasts, she dealt with it in her customary matter-of-fact way. She spoke, as I recall, about how, during the process of dying, the higher self and the double wrestle free of the bodily sheaths. On the night of the Anointing we had experienced the power of the higher self as it detached itself from the bodily sheaths and showed its striving to become an image of Christ. On subsequent visits I experienced the double in its cold subterranean nature. Generally, in the rough and tumble of everyday life, everything is mixed and muddled. Only occasionally do we get glimpses of these extremes of our nature. What we see in each other (and ourselves) is a mixture of the most noble spiritual qualities and the basest aspects of our lower nature. Yet at certain times, such as dying, these different qualities can stand out in stark relief, and this can be confusing and even frightening – as well as uplifting. So, when this happened to me, I was grateful for Evelyn's wise counsel. It gave sense and meaning to the experience.

Each death is of course different. I suppose there are as many variations as there are people. So it is not surprising that the second death that I experienced, in 1989, bore little resemblance to the first. The person who died on this occasion was an even closer acquaintance, although we had drifted apart a few months previously. In fact I didn't know about her death until a few hours after it had happened. So, whereas I had experienced the first death from close proximity, I observed this one from afar. And, whereas the first experience was essentially an experience of the dying process, this was an experience of bereavement. And, whereas my 'mother-in-law' had been happy and prepared for death, I understood that this other friend had been bitter and full of fear in the months before she died. She hadn't been so well prepared to die.

My personal experience of the two deaths also contrasted greatly. The first death was, for me, a mighty external event. Even though I was perhaps closer to the dying lady than anyone else in the final days (perhaps with the exception of the nurses in the hospital), I felt that it was essentially taking place outside me. It felt, so to speak, as though I was being introduced to spiritual and cosmic secrets. In fact, at about the time that my 'mother-in-law' died, I was impelled to go to the top of Primrose Hill. It seemed to me that I had witnessed her soul ascending into the heavenly world. The second death, on the other hand, was, for me, a deeply inward event. Whereas my experience of my 'mother-in-law's' death widened my being, this was an experience of inner intensification. In the first few days I was overwhelmed by feelings of sadness, grief, guilt and remorse. But this soon gave rise to an equally powerful period of peace and stillness, which I spent largely alone, in a state of inner contemplation.

Evelyn's counsel during the first death had enabled me to make sense of an experience that I didn't fully understand. On the occasion of the second death, she was again selflessly at hand. But now it was not so much understanding that she gave but emotional and moral support, and that is what I think I needed. In fact I can't specifically remember anything that Evelyn said on this occasion. The words were not so important. Instead I have retained a strong sense of her presence. It felt as though, throughout the bereavement process, she was there by my side – a strong and courageous companion, indeed, to accompany us in times of need.

June Leingang
London, England

Evelyn helped me meet a very evil situation by going to the guardian angels. She was the first to encourage me to ask for help from guardian angels. And she has greatly helped me in a physical illness caused by stress.

Evelyn gave me the comfort I could find nowhere else, and as a result I have become faithful to studying anthroposophy and am going through esoteric training now.

I wish Evelyn peace now.

Joan Maestrini
Bournemouth, Dorset, England

Evelyn helped me with my understanding of anthroposophy and myself when I attended one of her week's study groups of *The Philosophy of Freedom*, also during my several other visits to Temple Lodge.

A few years ago she invited me to accompany her and her sister Janet to the Goetheanum to see the *Four Mystery Plays* and arranged for us to stay in the students' home.

I very much appreciated her care for my wellbeing.

Cath March
London, England

Saving the Angel: how Evelyn Capel inspired a puppet show and saved my sense of humour.

I first met Evelyn when the Empty Space Theatre Company used Temple Lodge for rehearsals in spring 1995. The arrangement was a bit of a compromise on both sides, but a mutual respect for space and values allowed sacred and profane activities briefly to coexist. Evelyn struck me immediately as the guardian spirit of the place, generating a rich sense of harmony, history and charm.

Towards the end of our stay, we brought in one large scenic screen, for which we had to make room in the store adjacent to the chapel. As we shifted boxes and bags, I saw a tangled mass of strings and what looked like some marionette controls. Having worked with puppets since the age of twelve, I had to investigate further, and I found bits and pieces of some six marionettes, tangled, disjointed, unfinished. One figure was more or less complete, a female figure in a blue dress, but the others were in pieces, painted a bright Caucasian pink and clearly short of a few limbs. Before we left, I asked Evelyn about the puppets – if she knew who had carved them and how they came to be there. She didn't know exactly but she told me of a time when there were puppet shows at Temple Lodge. (Isla Bourke has since uncovered documentation of the British Puppet and Model Theatre Guild's shows and workshops at Temple Lodge in 1977.) I asked Evelyn if I could take away the abandoned bits and pieces of puppets, as I had an idea for a story involving a culturally diverse group of characters. She was most enthusiastic and encouraging, and I made a time to come back and visit her once the figures were finished.

Struggling and juggling freelance projects, I started work on the puppets. After a few weeks I took over the half-finished crew with some half-baked ideas for a show, wondering what Evelyn would make of it all. One of the characters I made was a West African woman, a doctor, carrying a medicine kit containing *sande hale* (Mende, 'women's healing'). I talked with Evelyn about the war,* about the seemingly impossible but necessary movements towards healing and regeneration. Evelyn was so patient, kind and understanding. I had been reading Michel Serres' *Angels: A Modern Myth*, and the idea of an angel crash-landing in the middle of an international airport came about. Evelyn laughed and speculated with me on the various roles that each character might play in saving the angel. Her gentle energy and enthusiasm were so contagious; she reminded me of my puppetry teacher, Violet Philpott, now in her seventies and still performing and clowning. I came away with a clear vision of how the show might go.

Since that time I've performed *Saving the Angel* many times for children's birthday parties, puppet festivals and most recently for a children's arts day at the Royal Albert Hall. I've also used the puppets in a classroom context, teaching languages to lower school secondary students. I

---

* The civil war in Sierra Leone, where Cath March had lived and worked.

would never have done this without Evelyn's support, advice and blessing.

Writing this short piece in the midst of a summer clearout, I am delighted to have the chance to thank Evelyn for saving my sense of humour and propelling me into action at a critical time. I know that she has inspired and motivated countless others and that this is a small contribution to a wider accolade; one feels a strange sense of a ripple effect. The idea of a female priest is still unfamiliar and perhaps uncomfortable to many, as is the idea of a female clown; yet although change may be uncomfortable, it is welcome if it takes us towards a more just and equitable society. Whatever our cultural differences, in a time of millennial confusion and spiritual crisis we all need a sense of humour and some sense of the sacred, a balance of responsibility and play, a sense that our smallest thoughts and actions can have a significant effect. In this briefest of tributes I would like to thank Evelyn for reminding me of this vital and ongoing balance that I seek to pass on to my daughter, family, friends and colleagues.

Janet Reid Jones
Aberystwyth, Ceredigion, Wales

In 1993 I was urged to make an appointment to see Evelyn Capel at her home in London. The clergy in the church of which I was an active member and choirmistress had never been sure of me. I was not prepared to agree that the Bible provided a blueprint for all moral behaviour, so was always a silent threat in Bible study classes. But when I had a series of very frightening 'occult' experiences with the dead over a period of nearly six months, the church treated me at worst as though I were evil and at best as if I were possessed and in need of deep cleansing and purifying. When I stopped attending they were only relieved.

Evelyn quickly and clearly saw my whole situation. She explained my experiences, said that I had been dealing with reality, not illusion, and for them so to misuse the word 'occult' showed the clergy's complete lack of knowledge. She rejoiced that what I had achieved was good and had been crucial for the one newly in the spirit world, that I was brave not evil, and that I had great understanding of the journey into this life and of the crossing into the spiritual world at death. I said that I hadn't, but she firmly insisted and showed me the way forwards, through strengthening my depleted etheric forces, to have courage.

I will never forget her and will always remain conscious of the help she gave to me. I think of Evelyn as my guide upon my way. Thank you.

Julia Tonge
Thornton-Cleveleys, Lancashire, England

I did not know Mrs Capel as well as many others; however, she has certainly had an effect on my life. During the summer of 1980 I was living in London and attended the Christian Community services at Temple Lodge for the first time. I had never seen a woman as priest before, having been brought up in the Church of England, which at that time did not allow women to become priests, but Evelyn's strength of presence and dignified bearing was such that I do not remember even feeling surprise as she conducted the service.

Later I came to know her. When she realised that I was returning to live in the north and that I was a writer, she put me in touch with mutual friends in Saddleworth, who were anthroposophists and also connected with drama. As I remember, we were all rather tardy in getting together at first but, on Evelyn's gentle insistence, we eventually did so, and friendships were formed that have lasted to this day.

The last fifteen months of my mother's life were spent in a geriatric ward, a fact that upset me greatly, but Evelyn was able to convince me that this experience – although sad for me – would be a great help to my mother and involved a balancing factor in her life, which she needed. Knowing this made it easier to bear. When my mother eventually died, I was not with her, something about which I felt guilty. I wrote to Evelyn about this, and she wrote back to me in very comforting words, explaining that love transcended space and time and that my mother would know that I *was* with her in every sense that mattered.

Many of the talks that I heard Evelyn give have stayed in my mind. She seemed able to express deep truths in a direct and memorable way. I wish her happiness in her final years.

Margaret Turner, formerly Repson
Moreton-in-Marsh, Gloucestershire, England

I first met Evelyn Capel in 1975/76 when she visited the Holy Land. It was my first meeting with The Christian Community and anthroposophy and proved to be a turning point in my life. Evelyn impressed me as a very strong, clear being, but also very warm and keenly interested in others.

Two years later I entered the Speech School, then in London, and for the first time stayed at The Christian Community in Hammersmith [Temple Lodge]. Evelyn was most warm and supportive during this time and later, when I had an eye operation in Bournemouth, I was astounded to receive a visit from her! Her conscientious care of those who attended The Christian Community was quite remarkable.

One lady who attended the church in Hammersmith told me a remarkable story about how Evelyn helped her husband who had had a stroke that had affected his speech. Evelyn visited him in hospital and at first used gentle persuasion to help him to speak, but then suddenly she raised her voice and said, 'I command you to speak!' and he did. Her incredibly strong will, imbued as it was with warmth and goodness, could achieve a great deal.

Evelyn was kind enough to present me with one of her books, entitled *The Christian Year*. I have found it most helpful and really appreciate the clear insights she brings.

Elizabeth Welziel
Twickenham, Middlesex, England

Evelyn helped me a lot when I returned from Rhodesia and found myself homeless. She gave me bed and breakfast at Temple Lodge until I was housed. I also enjoyed her talks on anthroposophy.

CHAPTER 6

Sacraments

Christine Carter
Brown's Hill, Gloucestershire, England

I am the daughter of Derek and Shirley Walters and niece to Eileen Hutchins. My parents worked at the Sunfield Children's Home where they met and married. They were committed anthroposophists and also members of The Christian Community.

During the Second World War they moved to Westwell Hall in Ilfracombe, Devon – where I was born. As it was war time and there were no Christian Communities nearby, my parents did not have me christened. However, when I was a year and a month old I fell from a first floor balcony onto an ash path; my parents saw me fly past a downstairs window! I appeared to have suffered no ill effects or injury, being well swaddled, but my parents now thought it imperative that I be christened. An SOS went out to The Christian Community and newly ordained Evelyn Francis (as she then was) undertook the journey to Ilfracombe and celebrated my christening on 19 November 1941. I believe this may have been her first christening.

Years later, after my marriage, we moved to Bracknell, Berkshire and would travel to Temple Lodge so that our children could attend the children's services. Then in April 1972 Evelyn Francis Capel christened our son Mark. We have fond memories of that day as Mark, who was about six weeks old, howled. Then mother played the lyre and immediately he became peaceful, as if hearing heavenly music.

Evelyn also conducted my entry into membership of The Christian Community.

I always admired her strength and determination and her knowledge, and found her lectures and written work interesting and thought-provoking.

I feel I have a really special connection, Evelyn having christened me in 1941 and, thirty-two years later, having christened my son.

Amy Croasdell
Northwood, Middlesex, England

Evelyn Capel
(Our Farewell Meeting in Temple Lodge with our much
loved Priest)

It was a special day
and all around
our voices hushed
not before the opening
of some final act
but so each one
could join the many voices
down the years
that sing their joy
of blessings she bestowed.

Of souls who felt
the angel wings around them
on their sacred journey forth.

The tender love of those
who joined in happy unity
to share life's tasks.

The youths confirmed in strength
and consciousness to find their
way into the adult world.

And tiny souls who
from their place in heaven
were welcomed into earthly life.

Evelyn dressed in her vestments, outside Temple Lodge, 1993 (photo: Alex Barlow).

Sometimes they came
to seek enlightenment
in their perplexity and doubt.

This quiet song we hear
from all who give her thanks
until the dawning day arrives
when Spirit Light
from Spirit Heights
will carry her on waves
of greatest joy and love
into the sacred Spirit Land.

Susan Davies, née Horsfall
Pinner, Middlesex, England

Evelyn in Africa, 1966

It was an African spring.
Monica, mother and grandmother,
loving our children small,
bringing golden days
to their infant imaginings
and balm to her deeper sorrow,
left us with sudden death.

Under that blue spring sky,
beneath the gazing face
of grey granite kopjes
clothed at their lichened feet
in leaves of freshly flamed
msasa, we buried her ashes.
Here, Evelyn, you spoke.

Now, in an English summer
thirty or more years on,
your words, in the turn of time,
have faded in our memory.
We think once more of the pain
unaching now in its age,

and thank you from our hearts
for the comfort and hope you gave.

Nim De Bruyne
Mynachlog-ddu, Ceredigion, Wales

Throughout my stay in Wales, which started with the founding of Nant-y-Cwm Steiner School, Michaelmas 1979, I've treasured Evelyn Capel's visits.

Starting with the Act of Consecration of Man at school, the many christenings, giving the sacrament of marriage or her lectures at Barbara Saunders-Davies, Evelyn came when asked, adapted herself to each situation, lifted it to an unforgettable experience.

For example: It was Kett's wish to be christened on the mountain. 'I will christen you, if you find the mountain,' said Evelyn. Halfway up Carningli (Mountain of the Angels, above Newport) a small plateau was chosen, and there Kett was christened, attended by his parents, godparents and friends.

I remember how Jason was christened at home. As Evelyn was about to leave, he ran down the stairs and hugged her so warmly.

In her lectures Evelyn drew from her long life's experiences, past and recent ones, like a meeting she had had on the Underground!

I remember how warmly she spoke of Casa Isabel in Portugal, a curative home, where she went to christen.

Jacqui and Martin Fisher
Penicuik, Midlothian, Scotland

You opened the door for us into The Christian Community. You shared with us your open-hearted, unassuming and uncomplicated way. We felt at ease and made welcome with the blessing of our daughter.

We hold a picture of contrasts in our memory from that day. It illustrates to us the ease with which you hold life in perspective. On the one hand, the picture was of a profound beauty and solemnity with which you performed the service to our young child. Then ten minutes later you were sitting outside in the courtyard in the sunshine, stroking your ginger cat with warmth and love: at ease in any realm, a contrast of the wisdom of years holding the significance of the entry of a baby into The Christian Community.

Thank you. We feel honoured for the short time we have known you.

Dr Branko Furst
Kinderhook, New York, USA

My first memories of meeting with Evelyn Capel reach back to the early eighties. Having finished my medical education, deeply disenchanted, I set out on a quest for something that, I intuitively thought, the art of medicine should be. After some travelling, I found myself in a big city: London. Having arrived there from Central Europe, where the cultivation of the old mystery streams has been reduced to mere memories, it was a revelation to be in a place teeming with New Age book shops, spiritual healing fellowships, colleges of psychic learning . . . and Temple Lodge.

Brought up as a Catholic, I had, even as a child, a deep reverence for the Christian Mass, the trouble being that my knowledge of Christianity was only at the elementary level as taught at religious institutions. Ever since I had learned about the idea of repeated earth lives, my interest had turned to the religions of the East, where this is a recognised fact. I even travelled to India and studied the Upanishads there. Only through theosophy was I able to inch my way back to Western occult tradition. It was at Temple Lodge, at a conference on Mystical Christianity, organised by Evelyn Capel, where I learned that, within Christianity, the idea of reincarnation also is a 'hot topic'. This, however, is not the Christianity that is found in tradition, but the Christianity that has been renewed from the deepest springs of the life of humanity. A seed had been planted for me that has grown, over the years, into the firm body of anthroposophy.

In due course I had several opportunities to visit Temple Lodge, attend the Mass and have a conversation with Evelyn.

On occasions, I would experience the divine Act of Consecration as a cosmic symphony, with Evelyn as the musician and the Heavenly Host conducting, the light streaming down in billowing sheets, shimmering in the radiant colours of the vestments, echoing with the mighty sound of the spoken word. The wine from the depths of the earth and the bread made with the help of the human hands were raised to the dizzying heights and rained in turn like the manna at the congregation. Truly, it was a memorable experience.

My last meeting with Evelyn was during her visit to our community in Harlemville, New York, in March of 1995. In the warm setting of a private home she spoke on the sacraments. So personable was her manner of discussion that one had the feeling of sitting privately at the Sacramental Consultation. Questions followed and, because of time constraints, not all could be answered. Before leaving for England, Evelyn had written me a personal note with a long discussion on the subject of the sacraments. It is one of my real treasures.

Christiane and Michael Lauppe
William Morris Community, Eastington, Gloucestershire, England

Evelyn used to come to South Africa in the sixties as there was no priest out there. Our two daughters were christened by her in Cresset House in 1964, when she christened at least six other children, all in a row! She also celebrated our wedding on 12 August 1962.

Back in Britain we have stayed a few times at Temple Lodge and spoken to her, although we did not have a close relationship. I admired her for her forthrightness and courage.

Her little book of verses, *Prayers and Verses for Contemplation*, I use frequently for my religion lesson: a lovely little book.

Dyana Rodriguez Hart
Hereford, England

In April 1985 Revd Capel baptised my son, Merrily (Mel), then one year old. This took place at The Christian Community, Temple Lodge, Hammersmith. My older son was at that time a pupil at the South West London Waldorf School.

About a week before the baptism, I met with Evelyn to discuss its meaning. Evelyn's perception, dignity and strength of spirit have stayed with me to this day. The light of her being seemed to glow from her, healing and calling forth a reciprocal courage and integrity in her interlocutor.

I have had little personal contact with Evelyn, but often felt her presence as a fount of comfort and support, and I am very grateful to her.

May she receive one hundredfold the support and caring she has given to others.

Beatrice Samuel
Stourbridge, West Midlands, England

In my mid-fifties (I am now eighty-one), when I was nearing the end of a lifelong (although chequered) career in a government office, living alone in 'digs' in London, and in a state of deep depression, I was taken by an office colleague to a Christian Community service at Temple Lodge, Hammersmith, where, of course, Evelyn was priest for many years.

I had been brought up as a member of the Church of England and was still nominally a member of that body, although by that time deeply disenchanted with its dogma and seeking some other focus for my spiritual life. I had never heard of a church called The Christian Community, nor of the Anthroposophical Society, and knew the name of Rudolf Steiner only as the founder of a certain type of school of which I knew precisely nothing.

I found that first experience of the Act of Consecration of Man totally overwhelming. Insofar as I succeeded in following it (which was not really very far), it seemed to overturn every tenet on which I had been reared. I arrived home on that Sunday in a state of complete exhaustion, feeling that I never wanted to repeat the experience. But something (I suppose now that it must have been my angel) made me go back . . . and back . . .

Gradually I began to take into myself the profundities of

the service, and under Evelyn's guidance began to overcome my reluctance to take on board the (to me) revolutionary concepts in the Act of Consecration and (later) to expose myself to the full teachings of Rudolf Steiner. Gradually I came to know Evelyn, not just as priest but also as a wonderful human being and a warm friend. (I hope she would agree with this!) And eventually, in retirement, I began to integrate myself fully with The Christian Community and the Anthroposophical Society here in Stourbridge.

Looking back now, it is possible for me to say that the meeting with Evelyn in Temple Lodge was a destiny meeting that changed the course of my life and one for which I shall always be deeply grateful.

I send her my warmest greetings and love.

Julie Toms and Neil Arbel
Kings Langley, Hertfordshire, England

On 11 July 1993 our son Christian Raphael was christened by Evelyn Capel. All christenings are indeed unique, but this one was very special because of the circumstances that surrounded it.

Christian was christened in the open air. In fact the ceremony took place in our back garden and was witnessed by over sixty friends, family and members of our community.

There is quite an extraordinary background to this event, and I feel it is necessary to honour both Evelyn Capel, as well as my son, by telling this story.

When I was four months pregnant with my third son, Christian, a scan revealed that he was to be born with bilateral talipes. This, of course, was a great shock to both myself and his father, Neil. I proceeded to devote the rest of my pregnancy to seeking out the best surgeon for my coming child as part of my preparation for his arrival.

Amazingly, it turned out to be easier to find a top paediatric orthopaedic consultant who specialised in feet (even although this was quite a task in itself) than it was to find a Christian Community priest who was willing to christen Christian.

Evelyn, 1960, with two children she had christened.

Whilst I was pregnant, a sense of urgency regarding the arrangements for a christening grew in me, a sense whose flames were fuelled by the knowledge that Christian would require numerous operations quite early in life. I spent much of my pregnancy in Park Attwood Clinic, and it was here that I developed a very clear vision of who Christian's godparents should be.

When I returned home, still pregnant, I discussed our choice of godparents with our residing priest. He objected to our choice on the grounds that we had opted for three godparents as opposed to the 'archetypal' two. To my priest this was a substantial problem, whereas to me the choice was one that was right and proper, in that my coming child was a being who would need as much 'holding' as possible.

When it became apparent that the christening would not go ahead unless we changed our minds regarding the god-parent situation, we decided to contact the Lenker. The Lenker stood firmly behind the view expressed by our re-siding priest, leaving us with the question – where to now?

Needing to turn over every stone, I rang a couple of other priests around the country who said they would have liked to help but felt unable to, because of the prevailing views on godparents. One of these priests advised me to contact Evelyn Capel.

By this point I was really losing hope as our baby was already three weeks old and we had not found a priest. When I eventually spoke to Evelyn on the telephone, I was amazed to find that she was totally willing to meet our requests.

Up to this point in time, the issue of a christening had become heavily laden with complications. My energy had been consumed in the efforts made to find the right way forward. Imagine, then, how revitalising and refreshing it was to encounter someone who possessed the confidence, courage and clarity of thought to commit herself to a deed that stood as a challenge to the prevailing beliefs. Evelyn's enthusiasm and confidence spread its effect throughout the following period and helped make Christian's christening a wonderful event.

We were not allowed to use the Christian Community chapel, so instead Evelyn agreed to carry out the christening in the open air of our back garden. The day was blessed by sunshine and a lovely group of differing people.

Amongst these people were individuals from The Christian Community who were then in conflict with each other over other separate issues but who on this day left behind their differences to take part in the christening of a wonderful child, a christening performed by a special priestess.

Even in the face of enormous opposition, Christ would have never turned anyone away. Evelyn stepped out of the shadow of dogma and in humility performed a truly Christian deed. For this I will be forever grateful to her.

CHAPTER 7

Pioneering

Kathleen Anthony
Harare, Zimbabwe

Evelyn had a great feeling for Zimbabwe (formerly Southern Rhodesia) and was always very welcome. She visited us quite a number of times, and almost always stayed in my house, holding Act of Consecration of Man services and giving lectures. On one of her last visits she christened four little children in my house in one afternoon. Two of them are now married.

Whenever Evelyn came here she spent some days with Jack and Maureen Kennedy at their farm in Mtoroshanga. She was very, very fond of them and their grown-up family. As for myself, I came to look upon her as a sister, so harmonious was our relationship.

She also christened my two children, Angus and Cynthia, who were then both at school. Later my daughter went down to Pretoria, South Africa, for her confirmation.

Many people here held Evelyn in high regard and still do, and it is sad that her visits had to come to an end. She was a great influence in my life, and that of my family, and in the lives of all those here who sought her advice.

Oda Thekla Bryan, née von Usslar
Cheltenham, Gloucestershire, England

I am writing to tell you [Evelyn] how much I personally – but also my late husband Cooper – owe to your lifelong work in The Christian Community and also to your many helpful and enlightening books and lectures over the years.

You may have forgotten – but I have not – what a decisive

influence your visit to Stuttgart in 1946 had, in the guise of an officer responsible for religious affairs in the Allied Control Commission for Germany.

You spoke to the congregation (or to a group of young people) in The Christian Community's temporary home next to the Waldorf School in the then Kanonenweg (now Haussmann Strasse). Whatever you said I cannot remember in detail, but it came as a breath of fresh air from beyond our isolated country and inspired us *and* was spiced with humour!

I had always felt a strong connection with the English language, already at school, but you were the link for me to fulfil my destiny in this country and I have always been very grateful to you for this. It is high time I express my gratitude in writing now at last, although I told you some years ago when we met at Temple Lodge.

Outstanding among holidays I have taken was my journey with a group you led in the early eighties to Greece and Turkey (Ephesus and sites of early churches). For this experience also I would like to give you a very warm *Thank You*!

Besides your decisive influence on me in my early twenties, during your 1946 visit to Stuttgart, I would like to record my appreciation of your work as a lecturer. The clearly structured form of your message, delivered in excellent German, was given with enthusiasm and conviction without a hint of mysticism and well spiced with down-to-earth (literally) examples and *humour*. It greatly impressed us young people. Your characterisation of the English people's initial contact with anthroposophy or The Christian Community via gardening and the compost heap, or St John's Gospel, was appreciated with amusement.

Later I was impressed by your open approach to anthroposophical truths and terminology in a religious context and your quite extensive lecturing activity at Rudolf Steiner House and all over the country, arranged by groups of the Anthroposophical Society in Great Britain, as a priest of The Christian Community. This was not a very common occurrence at that time and your style was much appreciated, particularly by 'newcomers'.

Dr Otto and Gertrude Burchard
Prien am Chiemsee, Germany

Gertrude and I have been asked to write something about what it meant to us in our life to meet you, and we think we can do that best by putting it in a letter to you.

We recently received from Pforzheim (Hans Heinrich's widow, Gundula) my parents' guest book. There we find that you, then Evelyn Francis, were a guest in my parents' home, first on 18 October 1937 and then again, 24 March until April 1938. I was at that time in my early twenties, three years younger than you, and was, of course, duly impressed by such a beautiful young lady from England, studying at the seminary of The Christian Community in Stuttgart.

I remember that on Saturday 23 March 1938 I persuaded you to save the train expenses and to ride behind me, on my motorbike, to Stuttgart. We had bad weather – snow and rain. Decades later you told us: there are things in life where *one* experience is sufficient, for example, riding on a motorbike!

In Stuttgart I saw the last Waldorf school performance of *Julius Caesar*, at a time when the school was already ordered by the Nazi authorities to close. I don't remember whether you saw this deeply moving theatre also.

Years went by, war and post-war, and then we were highly delighted to meet you in Pretoria. We are very grateful that you prepared and held the confirmation of two of our five children: Friederike in 1965, together with Cynthia Anthony from Southern Rhodesia (now Zimbabwe), and Christian in 1966 – in Cresset House! And we remember well the celebration of the foundation of The Christian Community in South Africa on 27 June 1965 in Johannesburg, in the presence of you and Dr Alfred Heidenreich.

There is one of your golden words that we often quoted: it is important that every spiritual effort is balanced by a material compensation. 'Eine geistige Leistung' must never be free of charge; otherwise Ahriman gets angry and does something to spoil that spiritual impulse. How true!

We remember also that we met in South Africa your late dear husband, Bert Capel.

Eileen Hartley
Chinhoyi, Zimbabwe

We had a very helpful anthroposophical group, which met every week in a town which was then known as Salisbury (now Harare).

Evelyn baptised my three grandchildren, Heidi Burdett who was born in 1973, Tanya Burdett who was born in 1975, and Christopher Burdett, who was born in 1980. On each occasion Evelyn stayed with us for a week or a few days.

When my husband retired, we went to a small farm in Marendellas. Evelyn showed great interest in all the farming activities. On her last visit she confirmed Heidi, Tanya and Bryan Waly, who later became Heidi's husband. This took place in Chinhoyi in 1990.

Rudolf Kirst
Kings Langley, Hertfordshire, England

I first met Evelyn in Cologne, soon after the end of the Second World War, when I was in my late teens. She was visiting various congregations in the occupied zones of the Western Allies in the guise of a colonel of the British Control Commission. This was a unique and truly pioneering task, which she had taken on with the intention of helping the scattered fragments of The Christian Community left after years of persecution and underground work during the Nazi regime. Evelyn struck my young mind with her courageous sense of purpose, which flowed through her lectures given in German.

When encountering Evelyn again in her later years, my perception of her inner sense of purpose struck me again forcefully. This sense of purpose focused on the celebration of the sacraments. It did not matter what the outer circumstances of this celebration were, what mattered was that the sacraments in fact were celebrated. She epitomised the commitment to her priestly duty to me in the following words, 'Who am I who, as a priest, can deny a sacrament to anybody who earnestly asks for it!' This sense of universality fitted perfectly my own perception of the tasks of The

Christian Community in our historical evolution of Christianity.

Sensing Evelyn's profound understanding of Rudolf Steiner's *The Philosophy of Freedom*, I recognised the inner connection between her highest task as a priest and what Steiner called 'moral intuition' and 'moral imagination'. She could only act as an individual out of her own moral intuition and imagination, and in doing so be independent from convention in general and also within her own movement. This was *her* Christianity, and this naturally caused tensions.

In the early nineties I watched Evelyn christen a child whom nobody else would christen because of some technical ruling. As this child was also denied the use of the local chapel, the christening was celebrated on the lawn in the garden of the parents, with a makeshift altar and altar picture, the candles being blown out by the wind. The setting did not matter; what mattered was that the child, who also had enormous health needs, was indeed christened. The large congregation that had gathered around this child was deeply moved.

It is not surprising that Evelyn needed her own setting, such as Temple Lodge, where she could be a host to the needy and the less needy, create her own cultural environment and remain an individual who could generate her own spiritual and social initiatives locally and, moreover, radiate out internationally.

She has made a unique contribution and given most dedicated service to our movements, to anthroposophy and The Christian Community worldwide.

Milena and Libor Nosek
Prague, Czech Republic (translation coordinated by the editor)
My wife, Milena, and I have accepted the offer to send you our best wishes and greetings from Prague, in grateful memory of our stay in London-Hammersmith when we accompanied our dear Mr Josef Adamec [priest of The Christian Community]. Those were beautiful autumn days of our

stay in your Christian Community, the Community you have built by means of your spiritual strength – the Temple Lodge!

The past, however, is slowly drifting away from us and is changing into a dream of memory, a dream of beauty. But man is not allowed to be at a standstill on any stage of his development, and we look with expectations at our future, and forward to our new meetings. We believe in our future cooperation concerning great spiritual assignments on our way to the fulfilment of the eternal Gospel of Christ.

When in England we had the opportunity to see – although briefly – the enthusiasm and sacrifice you devoted to your life's work. Thank you!

With many wishes for everything good and beautiful,

Charles Edward Oduro
Accra, Ghana

I, Charles Edward Oduro, first met Revd Evelyn Capel in London, at Temple Lodge, 51 Queen Caroline Street, Hammersmith, when I was in transit from Australia to Ghana in 1982. I had then gone to Australia for a mineral exploration course, for I was a geophysicist and geologist.

While in Australia I had the opportunity of meeting Anthroposophical Society members in Perth for a few times during their meetings to study spiritual science books. This generated my keen interest to listen to lectures on anthroposophy in London on my way back to Ghana.

I wrote to the Society in Great Britain to furnish me with information or a timetable of lectures for the general public or for members, and to help me get cheap accommodation for a few days, since I was then not financially strong.

When I arrived in London I had first to put up at a hotel before visiting Rudolf Steiner House. I was not observant and did not see a note for me on the notice board. That evening I had the opportunity of listening to lectures being delivered by anthroposophists. I was also lucky to be allowed to take part in an evening programme in eurythmy.

Apparently Revd Capel had previously come to Rudolf Steiner House to make a notice to be put on the notice board inviting me to come to Temple Lodge. It was on the next day that one of the members at Rudolf Steiner House reminded me of the notice, for he said I had been invited to Temple Lodge. He showed me how to get there.

I met Revd Capel and her husband and some friends at the Lodge. She offered me accommodation for the next two weeks for which my financial strength could carry me. During that fortnight, I had a great opportunity to learn much from Revd Capel. She took me and others in her own car to a museum and explained every bit of various paintings to us. She showed us pictures of old paintings, the landscape, buildings, etc, and the modern type of paintings, and the significance of the differences.

During the evenings I was permitted to join a study group, and I remember at that time Revd Capel used to explain the contents of *The Philosophy of Spiritual Activity* to the group. We were studying the contents of the book. She offered me the chance of asking her all sorts of questions, including those on reincarnation, Christ's appearance on earth and His second coming, the end of the world, and other questions from the Bible. In all these she gave me answers that added to what I had been reading. She was indeed helpful to me. She was very kind to me.

I returned to Ghana within the fortnight and, if I am permitted to say so, then I would say an anthroposophical or karmic relationship had been established between us. I used to write to her letters in which I continued to ask more questions and to which she wholeheartedly replied with answers. She gave me, and sent to me, many anthroposophical books by Rudolf Steiner, and some of her own books.

My wife had been blessed with the gift of the Holy Spirit. A spiritual message came to us to commence church activities way back in 1986. We were able to build a small church on a small piece of land in front of our house. However, the number of church members increased beyond the capacity of the building. We decided therefore to seek help for purchasing a larger plot of land for a commodious church building. Spiritual work like healing and relief from human suffering had been going on in our church, but the way of conducting religious ceremonies or cultus or, say, baptism, holy communion, marriage ceremony, burial of the dead, observance of Christmas, Easter, etc, posed a problem to the church because we did not know how to go about it, and we did not want to copy the pattern that had been adopted by the orthodox churches like the Presbyterian, Methodist, Wesleyan and Roman Catholic. Ours was a purely spiritual church and we wanted something that was spiritual.

I wrote to Revd Capel about the problems we were facing and how to get assistance from The Christian Community. We had also wanted to attach a Steiner school (Waldorf school), a biodynamic farm and a Steiner clinic to the church. I discussed these with her in my letters to her. She finally decided to come to Ghana to learn about the situation and to find out the way to assist us.

She came to Ghana in the last week of February 1993 and left in the third week of March. She left us with memories of love, for, when she was with us in our church, everybody shook her hand as a sign of love and appreciation for her visit. She granted the elders and the clergy of the church an audience for discussion of our problems and plans.

She willingly conducted our wedding ceremony (C. E. Oduro and Salome Agyarewa) and bound us together as man and wife in the name of the Father, the Son and the Holy Spirit. That day, 13 March 1993, was all joy and happiness for all of us, including herself. She preached to us in our church on several occasions and, when she went back to London, she left in our memories great love, respect and deep appreciation.

When the news spread that Revd Capel was coming to Accra (capital of Ghana) again, membership of our Church, called Jesus Christ Community Church (JCCC), suddenly increased. Her arrival again in Accra in 1994 generated fresh joy and elation. She continued to teach us both in our church and at the place where she was residing.

We repeated our plans and objectives to her. We have two Emerson College trained and qualified Steiner school teachers and one trained and qualified biodynamic farmer, to be able to start something.

We asked her whether it would be possible for her to get financial assistance from some donors or benevolent societies for us to begin to put our plans into action.

Even though she said she could not be sure, she said she would try to do something. And from her actions and speeches we could see that she herself was particularly interested in getting these things through, i.e. seeing to it that the land was bought, the church was built and functioning, the Steiner school was built and running, the biodynamic farm was producing, the clinic was practising and that the Anthroposophical Society of Ghana had obtained permission from Dornach and was operating.

We took her to see the land we intended to purchase from Opah Village Chief and Elders. She was happy about this land at the suburb of Accra. Fortunately, through her assistance we got financial help to purchase a ten-acre site. The final documents are yet to reach us from the sellers and owners of the land.

Rumour spread that Revd Capel was coming to visit us for the third time in 1996. Even though we were anxious and happy to meet her again, we felt that she was stretching her energy beyond what we thought should be her limit. This was because the heat in Accra was too much for her and that she could not walk with vitality without help. However, this did not materialise; only the announcement of her retirement.

In reality, we, the JCCC members, know that Revd Capel has our plans at heart and, if she were younger, we believe she herself would have taken upon herself to accomplish the plans and the objectives. We believe also that she is still behind our objectives in her thinking, soul and spirit.

It is our fervent hope that somebody, either in The Christian Community or in the Anthroposophical Society in Great Britain, will continue from where Revd Capel left off

Evelyn in Ghana, 1994.

in body, i.e. to visit us in person and feed Revd Capel with information on the stage we have reached.

Indeed Revd Capel is our godmother, spiritual mother, confidante, adviser, teacher, priestess, inspirer, helper and great friend. Please, send our love, the love of the entire membership of Jesus Christ Community Church in Ghana, to Revd Evelyn Capel.

Eva Oliveriusová
Prague, Czech Republic

I met Revd Evelyn Francis Capel only for two brief periods. The first time was when she came to visit Revd Josef Adamec shortly after the Second World War, as a young priestess. I adored her with the enthusiasm of a seventeen-year-old girl. In 1995 I had a discussion with her in London when I attended the Act of Consecration of Man. It was a very short talk concerning the situation of The Christian Community in Prague, briefly after Josef Adamec's death.

I have also read some of her works, which, for me, are in a true sense a modern anthroposophic feeling and view of and for man, world and Christ.

Would you be so kind as to give her my thanks for what she has done for people and my wishes of the strength we all need so much when the last period of life here on earth approaches.

Nancy Poer
Placerville, California, USA

Evelyn Capel was a special friend and colleague although I did not know her in England. We met when she lectured here in Sacramento two or three times in the 1970s. I found her lectures, like her writing, clear and refreshing. While wading through convoluted sentences translated from German is one way to strengthen the will, as an American I truly appreciated the insightful lucid way she wrote of spiritual matters directly out of the consciousness soul. A devotion to the word and the beauty of language are also present in her wonderfully direct style.

As a mother of six children, I began with her book *Growing Up in Religion*, which I found most inspiring and supportive. In meeting with mothers' groups, I found her warm and sympathetic even although that was not her own life experience.

As a founder of Rudolf Steiner College and faculty member there, and also one involved in community birth and death work, I found occasion to speak with Evelyn on many issues we shared. My last meeting with her, we arrived at the home of the Kimballs just as Ilse Kimball (Rudolf Steiner's youngest eurythmist) died. It was good to share that experience with her.

I appreciated Evelyn's grit and fortitude, and the English folk soul, yet nonetheless she put her own particular stamp on these traits. She was unflappable on any subject and most often had a seasoned and considered viewpoint to offer.

It is wonderful that she had the courage and destiny to become one of the first women priests for The Christian Community, to make a woman's place in the religious movement a reality.

I deeply value our connection and look forward to our continuing relationship in Michaelic work for the end of the century and beyond.

Revd Julian Sleigh
Camphill Village, Kalbaskraal, South Africa (Leader of The Christian Community in South Africa)

Evelyn Derry, as she then was, had a major impact on the course of my life. In 1962 her husband had recently died, and a friend in South Africa suggested she should get away for a holiday and visit South Africa, a part of the world that she had not yet come to know. This coincided in an amazing way with my wish to become a priest of The Christian Community and to serve in South Africa, if possible at the Camphill Village that my wife and I were planning to found. I felt I had a calling for the priesthood, but I had no idea how to go about it. I rejoiced when I heard that Evelyn was coming; I knew her name and some of her books.

Soon after she came to Cape Town, she visited the Camphill Centre near Hermanus where I was working, and we
met for the first time. It was a rainy afternoon, and when I
arrived at the house where she was staying, her first words
were, 'You sit down and I will bring you a cup of tea.'

Evelyn didn't have a holiday. Her days were filled with
consultations and services, with visiting people and holding lectures. By the time the three or four weeks were over
and she was about to move on, she had made a wide circle
of friends whom she had impressed with her knowledge
and courage. For many who had met The Christian Community for the first time, it was now something to aim for.

Evelyn opened the way for me and introduced me to the
Seminar in Stuttgart, and my path to the priesthood became
clear, so also that of Heinz Maurer.

In those days South Africa seemed a very long way away
from Stuttgart, and the idea of sending priests there was
seen by the leaders in Germany as being missionising to the
natives at the ends of the earth. But Evelyn knew exactly;
she had summed up the situation and the potential for our
work: the way we could cover the areas of Cape Town and
Johannesburg if two of us would come forward, the kind of
programme that was likely to succeed, the way to handle
the finances, and the way to be tactful towards those who
were active in the Anthroposophical Society.

After our ordination and induction in 1965, Evelyn was a
regular visitor. She knew how to admonish and encourage,
and the work soon took root in this new soil.

Evelyn was our mentor for many years and remained a
precious friend. Not only could I learn a great deal from her
about The Christian Community and about the priesthood,
but I admired her incredible grasp of *The Philosophy of Freedom* and her wide experience in pastoral care and adult
education. In her active years she was in every respect a
pioneer, ready to learn from her situations and to find the
way to penetrate them with a true impulse. Never was humour far away; there was always an anecdote to enliven her
thought.

Evelyn in Cape Town, South Africa.

She was highly practical, but she was equally aware of the need to show respect for people. 'I have learned in South Africa,' she said, 'how important it is to remember the names of the children of the people I meet, and also of their dogs.'

Maria Fernanda and Fritz Wessling
Seia, Portugal

Evelyn came all the way to Portugal to baptise our two younger children, and on both occasions she also baptised children of other friends. One may think that there is nothing remarkable about that; however, that is not the case. As we had come from Germany, and having already had two children born and baptised in Stuttgart, we first contacted The Christian Community there, to try to get someone to come – without success! However, as soon as Evelyn heard about our wish to have our third child baptised, she immediately made herself available. Not only did we have a lovely ceremony, where she baptised our child and two others, but on that same day (8 May 1989) she held the first ever Christian Community service in Portugal.

The second time Evelyn came to us (12 May 1991) it was again for the christening of our and others' children. That time we had a very enriching talk with her about what to do when someone dies in the Community. Our Community being young, we had not yet had to cope with such questions, but what she gave us helped later, when the situation arose in our midst.

What Evelyn gave by coming all the way to us was a real gift, one we shall never forget, and we carry that very warmly in our hearts.

We wish you much success with your endeavours and hope you will have enough contributions to do justice to Evelyn's magnitude!

CHAPTER 8

Books and Publishing

Anon 2

Although I only met Evelyn Capel briefly at the Christian Community guest house in London (Temple Lodge), where I stayed overnight, I have found her book *Studies in Christian Meditation* very helpful. For many years now I've used the book as a basis for inner work, finding the images she describes, and the various paths of meditation, enlightening and also a great support through difficult times.

Sevak Gulbekian

Managing Editor, Temple Lodge Publishing, London, England

My association with Evelyn Capel and the publishing work at Temple Lodge began in November 1989. Evelyn has always valued the written word, seeing it as an integral complement to the spoken word. From the beginning of her involvement with anthroposophy and The Christian Community, she has written many diverse works – several of which are considered classics of their kind (see, for example, *Growing Up in Religion*, more recently published as *The Mystery of Growing Up*, and *Thinking About Christianity*).

Evelyn's late husband, Bert Capel, began printing and publishing books at Temple Lodge in the 1980s. Following his death in 1986, this earliest incarnation of Temple Lodge Press came to an abrupt end. It was restarted, together with the attempt to continue printing 'in-house', by John Lees in 1987. I came to assist John in 1989. Following John's departure in April 1990, the company was re-launched under the new name of Temple Lodge Publishing. The in-house printing was discontinued and the focus was put on publishing.

When I first arrived at Temple Lodge, I can remember with great fondness Evelyn's occasional forays into the publishing office. She would sit in an armchair in the corner and speak forcefully about the importance of books in disseminating the ideas of Rudolf Steiner and a renewed Christianity. Evelyn is by nature a pioneer and had an appropriate pioneering attitude to publishing esoteric books. She knew that it was unlikely that there would be any profits from such publishing – and on the contrary that each book had to be funded separately. (This was refreshing from an author; they often have unreal expectations!)

On settling on a theme for a new book – often in response to a specific request – Evelyn would visit her long-time friend Miss Parton (whom she always addressed formally out of respect) and dictate many pages in a single sitting. After a few weeks she would return triumphantly to the office clutching a new manuscript. But once the book was written, she generally had little further interest in it – instead looking forward to the next project. Of course, she was pleased if a particular book had proved to be useful to one or another person, but she herself would never reread her own books.

Evelyn is perhaps one of the last remaining 'greats' from her generation of anthroposophists. I never had the privilege of meeting Adam Bittleston, John Davey, etc. To have known Evelyn, however, in all her dignified, gracious, yet powerful and choleric glory, has been a valuable gift in my life. Although she is now no longer able to work outwardly, the impulse she has given countless people in the past will continue to work into the future. For myself, I can say with certainty that the burgeoning publishing work at Temple Lodge would not be a reality without her original impetus.

Peggy Hall
Oxford, England

I have great pleasure in sending appreciation and gratitude to Revd Evelyn Capel for many of her books, which I have read over and over again during the past twenty years or so.

I found especially valuable, in discussions with students and when introducing them to Dr Steiner's books, the following, which the students found very accessible when reading aloud to me from them: *The Christian Year*, *The Timeless Storyteller* and *Thinking about Christianity*. Several of the students were not Christians but found her books interesting and stimulating. Her circular letters, *Companions of the Inner Life*, were of great comfort to me over the years.

With much love to Evelyn from my husband (Gerry) and myself.

Stella Parton
Kew, Surrey, England

I met Evelyn Capel in the early seventies, a short time before my father died. I shall never forget her great kindness. My father was very compassionate and caring but did not belong to any church. Evelyn offered to give him a Christian Community funeral and memorial service. I joined The Christian Community (London West) shortly afterwards. Evelyn has given me great help in understanding Christian Community theology and expanded my understanding of anthroposophy considerably over the years.

For nearly twenty years Evelyn came to my quiet home and dictated to me what were to be her books and articles. Active as she was, with little time to spare, we decided that it was quicker to put shorthand aside, and I typed as she dictated.

I grew to know her well and tried to provide an oasis where complete concentration was possible. She encountered higher realms of inspiration at times, and it was a very real privilege to help her in this work.

Born under the sign of Aries, Evelyn Capel has shown in her life and work many strong characteristics associated with this powerful sign: pioneering, courage, determination and one-pointed devotion – the latter in her case related to the renewal of Christianity and Rudolf Steiner's anthroposophy. In all her writings, she gave full credit to Rudolf Steiner, where appropriate.

Today I pray deeply for her and in tribute to her attach a copy of her poem given personally to one seeking counsel and now published in her book *Prayers and Verses for Contemplation* (Floris Books, Edinburgh, 1992, reproduced by kind permission).

Forgiveness

Not on the trees of Paradise
The strangest of fruit bears seed.
It is not the apple of life nor knowledge freed.
Its seed will never scatter in that garden,
But is planted in the dark of earth
The place where Man is alone from birth.
But see, the immortal one is with him
Who knows the lonely cross,
Who withstands the fear of loss,
Who sheds unceasingly the light of grace.
The cross-tree is planted on earth
Bearing strange fruits of grace,
Stronger than the apple of strife,
Tasting of fresh, unimagined life,
The fruit of forgiveness
Both received and given.

William Smirthwaite
Hove, East Sussex, England

I first met Evelyn Capel in the late fifties at Benen House. From that moment I was greatly impressed by her clear and firm manner of talking about quite difficult subjects so that they could be pondered over and understood.

In the main I have benefited greatly from the books she has written, and over the years have read and reread them as the constant source of inspiration that they are. It is like having a friend and counsellor always ready to advise and guide about the greatest mystery that life can hold.

This source of wisdom flows from a lifetime of devoted service that Evelyn has so faithfully given to the Christ Being, not only in word but in deed.

Alan White
South Croydon, Surrey, England

I have known Evelyn Capel for quite some time and have received helpful letters from her on aspects of Rudolf Steiner's work. My mother used to receive *Companions of the Inner Life*, a series of meditations on the Bible and other spiritual sources. After my mother's death, I discovered some of these meditations, which I found most helpful in the method and content of their thinking. I would very much like to see this series published in its entirety, if possible.

Nelson Willby
London, England

Evelyn Francis Capel is a pioneering spirit, having been one of the first women priests in Great Britain. Her entry and work in the priesthood of The Christian Community church go back to her ordination in 1939. An important part of this work has been her writings, which have entered deeply into the hidden aspects of esoteric Christianity. Having studied history at Oxford, she has combined a knowledge of the world with her academic background and the Christosophy of Rudolf Steiner to create a life dedicated to her calling as a priest with a devotion to her congregation underpinned by a social impulse answering to the needs of everyday life.

Her literary output is upwards of twenty-five titles, including numerous articles ranging in content from works on the sacramental life, biblical studies, insights into the cycle of the year, cultural history, philosophy and education to plays, prayers and verses. When it comes to the writing itself, the words just seemed to flow from her in what seemed to be, in the finished result, effortless prose. An interesting sidelight that supports this view has been her method of writing. She dictated the contents of her books to her secretary [Stella Parton], who immediately typed them. This freed Evelyn to speak with appropriate animation and even passion as she felt the ideas arising in her soul and she could express herself without being encumbered by the physical process of writing. It was as though she touched a higher realm in this process. This accounts for her fresh, flowing style, which reveals a deeper aspect to her life that did not, in my experience, usually come to the fore in everyday conversation.

In what follows, space permits only one example of the quality of her writing. It comes from her book *Pictures from the Apocalypse* and deals with the great question of transformation. I quote from pages 74 and 75:

How is it that angels appear so often in the Book of Revelations handling forces of destruction? . . . Permanence belongs only to the material world. In material terms value is set upon what does not disappear and it is only in this area of existence that that which is long lasting is produced. When the forces from beyond the Earth are at work, there is waxing and waning. The clouds come and go, the seasons rise and fall, there is blossoming, seeding and fading in the fields. The Heavenly forces from beyond the Earth do not work to preserve, but to renew. Unless there is fading, there cannot be renewing. Wherever in the Book of Revelations Heavenly forces invade Earth existence, the angels who are of the Heavens do not preserve, they are occupied with destroying and renewing ... What is destroyed in the material region rises up to new life in the region of the vital forces. There should be no sense of tragedy in the world processes which are handled by the angels. For every picture of destruction there is one of vital shining in another sphere.

In this fine insight, the principle of transformation – the dying and becoming of human and earth existence – is so clearly brought out and developed. This is done within the context of the pictures of the Apocalypse, depicting the angelic world in its power to destroy but with equal authority to renew.

Here, too, we can grasp the deeper meaning of renewal for human destiny. As our earthly life wanes and ebbs away, what otherwise would imprison one in rigid material forms is dissolved, releasing the inner life and freeing the soul to the gradual realisation of its deeds of service. For we too are led by our angel and as our life wanes and ebbs away all that has been given in selfless service will be renewed on a higher level for ever greater deeds for humanity's evolution.

CHAPTER 9

Personal Tributes

Regula and Roland Aegler
Münchenstein, Switzerland

We cannot think of Evelyn Capel without remembering her special devotion and talent with children. We met her for the first time on the occasion of her visit to Johannesburg in 1974 or 1975. She was invited to our home for dinner. Our three-year-old son, Thomas, was very peculiar with guests he did not know. Perhaps he would say, 'I do not like you and you better go home again,' as he had been doing this with other guests. Not knowing Evelyn and her reactions, we just hoped that Thomas would be in an acceptable mood.

Nothing of the sort happened. Thomas was so pleased when Evelyn said hello and started to chat with him that within two minutes he was, to our great surprise, sitting on her lap – something he had never done before. There must have been hidden threads between them.

Evelyn Capel was a big help to us in educational and philosophical questions we had at that time, and we strongly regretted that her visit was so short.

Revd Peter Allan
Stroud, Gloucestershire

During the clear nights of March and April 1997, many of us will have looked up at the Hale-Bopp comet, gazing at this brilliant traveller through the star-filled sky. Coming from the far limits of the solar system, the comet spoke to that in each of us which longs to remember its heavenly origins.

For several weeks its shining head and far-flung tail were a truly wonderful sight.

Whenever Evelyn was at her best, her light-filled words enlivened the chosen theme in a similar kind of way. Just eight or nine years ago, during the Holy Nights here in Gloucestershire, she spoke on the theme: 'Christmas, a time of open doors'. She pointed to Christ's own development and showed that our understanding of Christmas, and of the Christian festivals, must equally develop further. This she related to twelve differing ways of coming to an understanding of the world and to the ideas and attitudes arising from these ways. She was in good form, and her story, overheard in the kindergarten she said, made a suitable point: 'You know, I wasn't always here, I used to be in heaven.' 'Yes so was I; I thought somehow that we'd met before.'

Because of distance, Evelyn and I did not often meet but there was mutual liking when we did. As it is with comets, her movements were unpredictable at times, but in one way or the other there was always a big *sweep* about them. I am very grateful for her awareness of the world as a single whole and for the fact that this has been understood and is now being worked on by others.

Our most recent meeting was in Wales, when parents had asked me to take a christening that she could no longer hold. Yet the evening before, she came to the meeting that was to prepare it, and then next day to the christening itself, taking part simply through the intent way in which she listened to the words being said. In the best sense something comet-like has always surrounded Evelyn, and it is the meetings where this showed that will remain in my mind.

Kevin Avison
Baughurst, Hampshire, England

I first met Evelyn Capel when she came to the small Curative Home School, where my wife and I worked at that time, to baptise our children. Subsequently, I attended a number of services and festivals at Temple Lodge, and Jane and I reconfirmed our marriage with the Christian Community sacrament which Evelyn conducted.

What moved me about Evelyn was her great sensitivity in the use of language for her sermons or whenever she spoke about the services. Her words always had a directness and immediacy, often a poetry, which gave a feeling of freedom to her hearers, something that seemed to come from an intense inner listening on Evelyn's part. Being in one of Evelyn's seminar sessions could be an intense experience because one was encouraged to move in one's thinking onto another plane from that of everyday talk. Not that there was anything of mystification or obscurity about her words, quite the contrary, but I often felt she was actively creating new vantage points from which one might enter reality from a previously unsuspected direction. It was a vivid experience. Similarly, her speaking of the liturgy had a life but also a clarity which is in the gift of very few.

Although our work led to us rather losing contact with Evelyn and developments at Temple Lodge during the ensuing years, each member of our family retains a strong and fond memory of Evelyn and her ministry. I am particularly grateful to her for this example of disciplined freedom of thought which I have been trying to apply to my work as a Waldorf teacher. Certain apparently passing remarks that she made have remained, years later, as active constituents in myself. Some years ago the *Anthroposophical Review*, as it then was, published a poem of mine. A note of appreciation from Evelyn was, and still is, the best encouragement anyone could receive, not so much as a poet but to continue the encounter that gave rise to the poem.

Thank you, Evelyn, for your resolution and clarity. Thank you for your service to the Word.

Michael Beaumont
London, England

I have just been thinking back on some of the memorable occasions in which I have participated during the years that I have had a connection with Temple Lodge.

There was the trip to Dornach to see the Mystery Dramas in, was it 1983? We all piled into Bert's minibus and then piled out again for a picnic at various places en route in France. It was a particularly hot summer, or so it seemed to me, yet we were able to make the most of events in Switzerland. The return journey took us back with a night in Troyes.

Then, just a couple of years ago, we made a trip with you to Prague. This was a real adventure because it was made very shortly after travelling restrictions to and in that part of Europe were lifted. The high point of this visit was a talk by Revd Josef Adamec about the Karlstein Castle. We were able to appreciate its significance all the more when we visited it the following day. I am sorry that you found it difficult to manage all the staircases and that you did not come up to the chapel with us. But nonetheless you got us there and back (to Prague, that is) in record time. The arrangements for staying the night en route always worked out perfectly.

I feel sure many people will have memories of journeys made with you, and I, for one, am grateful that they were possible – I might not have had such adventures otherwise!

Trips to South Wales with you 'on business' could also be quite adventurous. I shall never forget trying to find the farm where the wedding was to take place. The landscape and all signposts (if indeed there were any) were shrouded in fog and mist. The couple, wedding guests and everyone (plus cats, dogs and farm animals) must have breathed a sigh of relief when we turned up on time.

On a more personal note, I still remember the occasion when I came to you with serious life questions. You very helpfully suggested I write an essay about choice; it might even have been connected with *The Merchant of Venice*, but I forget the details. My apologies, but I still have to get around to writing or showing you anything. However, having thought a great deal about the choices one has to make in life and the reality of choice as such, one begins to value the fact that differing situations require choices to be made. They seem to be stepping stones across streams on the road to freedom. Thank you, Evelyn, for helping one in trying to find the true relevance of Christianity today.

Peter Bridgmont
Chrysalis Theatre, London, England

Evelyn Capel has always been for me a slight enigma in her role as a priest. For both the responsibility of establishing a centre at Temple Lodge and certain necessary constraints placed on her in her role in The Christian Community often caused me to wonder about her career had it been outside the priesthood. Although carrying out her duties with sound judgement, diligence, and often extreme kindness, her powers as a speaker, her knowledge of the secular world, her capacity to intermix morality and understanding in any given situation, seemed to place her deeper into world affairs than she was able to attain within the Community.

I could imagine her in the world of politics or any powerful social organisation that would demand from her a grasp of the moral and pragmatic attitudes demanded from situations that are so much the part of public life today.

I always felt certain remarkable talents lay within her which could not be used fully and a driving will that had the capacity to carry out projects that her present destiny did not lay before her.

A wise, humorous, talented lady who laid down what could have been a satisfying worldly career in order to bring to those around her comfort and knowledge.

Margaret Daunt
Wallingford, Oxfordshire, England

We first met at a Wrekin Trust conference, the one Sir George Trevelyan asked me to start by singing! You then asked me to work for you and we had many subsequent sessions, 'The Hierarchies' and others, where Sir George and I worked with words and voice and harp. And when your dear husband left us, I came and sang the oldest known version of the Lord's Prayer as a little requiem for him. And your wonderful brave control ended when you said goodbye to me. You wept, and this is necessary in countering grief, as I know only too well as I have wept so much myself. My wonderful Brian went on his way in March last year [1996]. You were able to answer questions for him, and you even came down here to see him.

We both loved your books, the splendid publishing venture and the excellent restaurant.

You enlarged my faith in the holy factor of sound, and through you I have been a music therapist for many years, working with drug addicts, schizophrenics, rejects from mental hospitals, and so on, as well as my solo work.

Brian and I loved the serenity you created in performing the rituals of The Christian Community. Everything you did contributed to the Community in your own unique and wonderful way.

With thoughts and prayers, and always love.

Elizabeth Flanagan, on behalf of all the family
Saddleworth, Lancashire, England

Evelyn was a facilitator before the word became common parlance. She has always had the capacity to arouse enthusiasm and initiative in people that they did not know they possessed!

We first met at the Keswick conference centre of The Christian Community [Woodford House], attending a drama course that she and Peter Bridgmont ran. The 'we' is my husband Desmond and our two sons, Alexander and Jason, and myself. The following year Peter was unavailable, and we found ourselves enlisted to run the course instead! Like Peter we were both trained at conventional drama schools but had not his advantage of training also at the Goetheanum! Nevertheless, for several years the course was our project and a wonderful expansion of our experience. We were also pressed into learning how to serve at the Act of Consecration of Man – no mean feat over the period of a week, although we had been attending services in Man-

chester. Evelyn's practical competence as priest complemented her great spiritual intellect. One was able to make
mistakes (having been thrown in at the deep end!) without
feeling one had somehow committed sacrilege. Honest endeavour and devotion were always recognised by Evelyn.

The next initiative that she encouraged was the confirmation of our two sons. This widened their social circle as well
as imparting considerable further religious knowledge during the period of preparation. On one occasion during
Jason's instruction (the difference in age of two and a half
years meant that Alex was confirmed first), it was agreed
that Evelyn would come north to stay with us for a few days.
Jason had a day off school, which I had not (I was teaching
at the time), and so he and Evelyn were alone for lunch. She
was most impressed by the local parkin cake topped with
fresh double cream that Jason gave her for pudding!

Shortly after Easter and the confirmation service came
the event that changed all our lives and that Evelyn and
Bert (her late husband) helped us through. In June 1976
Jason was hit by a car whilst crossing the road in our village
and very severely injured. Bert drove Evelyn up the next
day to be with us at the hospital, where Jason was to stay for
five months, for three of which he remained virtually unconscious. Evelyn came several times during that period,
helping us through a trauma that no words can describe.
She advised us on Rudolf Steiner's insight into such blows
of destiny and gave us books to read that we had not already encountered. Suffice it to say that Evelyn's help, both
then and in the ensuing years of Jason's disability and rehabilitation, has sustained us in a way that no amount of
thanks can express. Each time Evelyn saw Jason she found
something positive to say about his progress. Needless to
say she is Jason's heroine.

The last time we were able to see Evelyn was at Temple
Lodge in 1995, shortly before her official retirement. It was a
flying visit – we were only in London for two days because
Jason decided that he must see the Elgin Marbles! His interest in art and painting was also encouraged by Evelyn. Such

rare visits are fraught with difficulties, but we were so glad
to see Evelyn even for a short time, especially in the light of
subsequent events.

Desmond's work in the psychiatric services in the NHS
as a lay therapist was always of interest to Evelyn. She
would telephone out of the blue and say she would like to
come up and stay for a couple of days in order to accompany Desmond to the hospital and observe his professional
activity. Such occasions were always precious and the ex-
change of ideas stimulating. My own work was cut short by
Jason's accident. I gave up teaching to look after him, but
was able to go back to doing the odd day's TV work after
1983. That was fun, and organising for Jason to be cared for
on an odd day or two was not too difficult.

But I wanted to do something more worthwhile, on however small a basis. The chance came when I contacted Manchester University's Extra Mural Studies Department and
asked the director whether I could organise a summer term
course on Rudolf Steiner. The answer was an encouraging
'yes'! The first two years I was able to invite eight different
speakers to come week by week. Needless to say, Evelyn
came as one of the lecturers and was as always wonderfully
encouraging and delighted with the initiative. The 'crunch'
came in the third year when the director said we must conform to the normal procedure now and have only one lecturer for the eight weeks. The local anthroposophical group
was subsidising the lecture courses by providing travel expenses and overnight accommodation over and above what
the university fee was. Most lecturers were coming from a
distance to do one lecture in a course. Who would be willing to travel to Manchester week after week to do seven or
eight evening lectures? Of course when Evelyn knew the di-
lemma she offered to come. Saved again! After that, others
came each summer, and the annual lectures on Rudolf
Steiner and his influence upon so many spheres of life have
gone from strength to strength.

Evelyn's legacy is incalculable. Those who have passed
through Temple Lodge have taken something of it out into

the world. She herself has travelled worldwide, spreading the work of anthroposophy and The Christian Community. She was always ready to take the sacraments to wherever they were needed. Her contribution to this field of endeavour is rich and enduring. Her books are a lasting testament to her spiritual inspiration. But it is her humanity, and her own love of humanity, that endures in one's memory. Her interest in all things; the picture of her in her dressing gown with her hair down brushing the cat; her laughter, which could break easily through her serious, intellectual nature; her friendship enduring across disagreements or misunderstandings; her greatness of soul throughout our long acquaintance; these will all evoke our love and admiration, and fondest memories of her for as long as we live.

John Flynn
Reading, Berkshire, England

One thing you often said has always stayed with me; it was your reiterated belief that Steiner's work was a *living* philosophy – and by implication not something to be kept sealed from the world. Debate and meetings were important but application of learning should be with and for people. You were an exemplar of this, always striving to give form and expression to new ideas (e.g. by arranging study groups, seminars, workshops and the like). In other words, you clearly lived with great energy and commitment that which you espoused – even in your later years. I suspect that much of the irritation and annoyance you are renowned for springs from your belief that others should do the same. I had enormous respect for your way of life as I watched you trying to move people, ideas and concepts forward. However, this way of being separated you to some extent from those around you.

You cared for the errant members of your flock when they were in need of help. You always had time for people – even for those perceived as 'difficult'. I was much taken with the story of your visit to Hammersmith police station to cajole the custody sergeant into releasing a member of the flock into your care. Your personal presence carried authority, and this helped you to perform such deeds; this was enhanced by your being an active member of the local community. Actions of this kind did not always meet with the approval of those around you, but you persevered in living your deeply held convictions. As a result, there will be many inarticulate, even irreligious, people who will remember you with gratitude.

Thank you for the many insights about our son, which helped ease his early life. You were the conduit through which he went to a Steiner school. I have always appreciated this, although you could not have anticipated how much the school would change. I appreciated your help and concern at the time, despite later misgivings. You may recall advocating that he should be sent to a school with a strong masculine input at a later date. For this also I shall always be grateful – the move took place and was important for him.

Your later years at work were not easy, and this saddened many of those who appreciated the years of devoted service you had given. But you valued what support you were given, and your spirit transcended physical difficulties. For you, at least, the drive to care for other individuals came from strong feeling, which led to appropriate action through will forces – just as Steiner described.

Well done, Evelyn. You have been a Colossus in the movement, and Steiner's models will live on through your teachings and example. Lest you forget, think of the many people whose lives you have changed and be aware of their admiration and gratitude. Salutations – with affection and respect.

Berenice Hereford
Mordiford, Herefordshire, England

Evelyn has been a dear friend to our family and, later, to my husband, over a period of many years: in the hill country, on the Shropshire, Montgomery borders and, later, in Herefordshire. During that time she has shared the joys and sorrows of our lives, both as priest and loving friend.

As a fairly new and young priest she stayed with us, sustaining us all, on the death of my young cousin, Barry. Barry had been learning biodynamic gardening and farming, as a student, at Sunfield, Clent. There he was found, by the care of 'Mummy Geuter', to have a heart condition, from which he died, aged eighteen years.

Evelyn conducted Barry's passing and funeral in such a way that we were able to feel it as a perfect completion of his life among us and as a prelude to a continuation for us all. This was an experience that has always been with us as a part of our whole: a rightness, made complete by Barry's humour and courage, clarified and demonstrated by Evelyn to us all.

There has been so much to enjoy and share with Evelyn: a humour always positive; the natural world about us; a simple meal; growing lives of children; colour, form and beauty; reverence and growing knowledge.

We know Evelyn as a spiritual leader of insight and inspiration: one through whom the living Christ is present.

Christ present through her celebration of the sacraments.
Present in her conversations; her writings; and her meetings with all kinds of people.
Present through her loving and wise help in times of perplexity and sorrow.
Present in her joyful sharing in times of happiness and achievement.
Evelyn has influenced my life through living as she has done and as she continues to do.
Through being herself; through being 'Evelyn'.
'Evelyn', an inspiration and loving guide to so many of us; humbly; in the name of Christ.

Alice Barton Karnes
Hillsdale, New York, USA

I first met Evelyn Francis Capel at Chrysalis, the home of Dr Basil and Christina Williams in Harlemville, New York, several years ago, just prior to her retirement. She was leading a workshop on *The Philosophy of Freedom*, her thoughts often entering into the subjects of 'free schools' and the moral dilemmas of physicists.

Just as Evelyn's discussion persisted with the difficult dilemmas I too had met, I was reassured and warmed to find such a worthy, concerned effort being made.

I was impressed with Evelyn's firm kindness of heart and a great presence of soul about her. We did a study of Leonardo da Vinci's *Last Supper* together and decided to attempt a book-writing session. She worked on the festivals; I attempted some artistic themes I had not attempted before and offered her a portfolio of work.

Evelyn seems to have led such a rich and supportive life, touching on such major tasks for The Christian Community.

Bernd Kassner
Witten, Germany

Entry in my diary, Saturday 31 January 1987:

'I passed through the gate and saw a big old house. A bookshop, a chapel, a restaurant. I rang the bell. Mrs Capel opened and gave me a warm welcome.'

One can easily imagine this scene – the Angels' Gate, the white house, the blue door, and who opens it. I of course could not.

I 'fell from the sky' two hours before at Heathrow, took the Underground, found my way through Queen Caroline Street and stood in front of the house, not knowing what to expect and whom I would meet. This will be my home for four weeks – I was then a journalist trainee working at our foreign correspondent's office in London – but what would my host be like? Imagine yourself far away from home, in a foreign country, lost in a big city, standing in front of an unknown house – and then, a warm welcome.

This was my first encounter with Mrs Evelyn Capel. Others were to follow – talks about anthroposophy, for example. And here it was again: she allowed me to 'knock on doors' and, if I did, she opened them, explained things that were behind them. She did not open all doors widely from the beginning – and I am grateful for that – so that I might stumble in and probably find myself in an unfitting room, a room with too big a size for me (and my then knowledge of anthroposophy), but she opened one or another 'anthroposophical door' I was knocking at and, yes, again gave me a warm and understanding welcome.

The 'prophecy' she made one evening, when I told her about the high rate of unemployment in Germany and my fears about getting a job after the end of my training, became true. 'No doubt you will get a job,' she said. I would not call this supernatural, but she obviously had an eye for the persons she talked to and listened to, for their skills as well as for their tasks they have to do in this life. A clear eye and a welcoming eye.

Now, ten years later, I do still remember clearly talks we had in those four weeks, the Act of Consecration of Man in the chapel (I became a member of The Christian Community in the meantime), one supper or another we had in the restaurant.

And if I may have a wish for her, it would be 'a warm welcome, wherever she is going to, and a door that opens upon her knocking'.

Paul Langston
Stapleford, Nottingham, England (trustee of Christian Community/London West and Temple Lodge Publishing)

The Christian Community and Temple Lodge have been a large part of my life over the last fifteen years. I know my mother, Phyllis, who died in 1990, would like it noted how Evelyn and Gladys Mayer helped her after the death of her seven-year-old in 1953. The main help was in the appreciation of the *reality* of the spirit world.

For me, her book *The Timeless Storyteller*, on the parables, was a most original and modern interpretation.

Working as a trustee at Temple Lodge I found Evelyn quite an enigma – very much a 'Margaret Thatcher personality'.

Without Evelyn and her late husband, Bert, Temple Lodge would not be part of The Christian Community today. Our main tribute must be to help in the developments at Temple Lodge.

Let me also add an appreciation of Cecelia Fisher, the [honorary] treasurer at Temple Lodge for many years. She is now ninety-five and, by choice, still living on her own.

Charles Lawrie
Portmadoc, Gwynedd, Wales

Evelyn Capel, the residing priest at Temple Lodge, emanated a contrast of earnestness and humour, her intelligence penetrating every circumstance, with trained imagination. I met her via the Mercury Arts household, and her readiness to support Gladys Mayer as an inspired speaker and artist. Many a vibrant watercolour of Gladys Mayer's adorned the walls at Temple Lodge. Evelyn and Gladys were both lady-ambassadors of anthroposophy in South Africa – and there was a deep bond of affection between them. Bert Capel, meanwhile, with his warmth and can-do attitude, enabled the link to grow – ferrying the exhibition (with artist and entourage) in his minibus and setting it up in the Frank Brangwyn Studio at Temple Lodge. It is said that when Bert Capel told Alfred Heidenreich, 'I want to marry one of your priests,' Heidenreich responded, 'Oh, yes. Which one?' 'There isn't much choice,' came the instant reply! But Bert's heart knew only too well its depths of love and respect for Evelyn.

When my father died young in 1976, he came to me in a dream. Appearing in some distress, he took a wig from his head and exposed himself as quite bald. The meaning eluded me then but the feeling of urgency led me to Evelyn. I always found her rock-solid on matters of practical occultism, and she swiftly guided me: it means he has not yet the wherewithal to form the necessary conceptions for his new environment of soul and spirit and he has come to you for help. Therefore, you should read to him, for example, from Rudolf Steiner's *Christianity as Mystical Fact*. So I did, light-

Evelyn with Bert Capel at Temple Lodge.

ing a candle and proceeding at the same time each evening for over a month. My father seemed to take interest as I tried to lift up the living conceptions of Rudolf Steiner's descriptions towards him, and to gain as time went on, and we inwardly approached the Baptism in the Jordan, a deepening tranquillity. Without Evelyn, I could not have done this.

Appreciating Evelyn's well-known ability as an authoritative speaker with a specially fine mind (no less evident in her fascinating and well-stocked library made over for others to use at Temple Lodge), I invited her to speak on occasions at Oxford and in London, and once to an unusual gathering in New Oxford Street, attended by Mathoor Krishnamurti of the Bharatiya Vidya Bhavan, in connection with Major T. Ramachandra (who helped to found the Dr Rudolf Steiner Education Society and the Anthroposophical Society of India). On this occasion, I found Evelyn's talk a little formidable for her mainly Hindu audience – but the challenge was unmistakeable!

Evelyn baptised three of my children, and the way the

light of the spirit shone into the little babes, strengthening them on their path into incarnation, as she made the priestly gestures above their infant brows, remains unforgettable. What a priest! And what a patron of the arts!

One of Evelyn's great loves was to set off in Bert's minibus to lead tours of Druid London, of which she had a very living conception. She knew the constant stream of music and worship that belonged to the Sun-cult of the Druid colleges of old – and this formed a background to her awareness of the metamorphosed cultus of the present. She was a Blake scholar and saw him clearly in this context.

A theme to which she gave typical profound attention, and which cannot be underestimated in its relation to the giving of the sacraments of the modern Christian Community, was the Second Coming. Said Dr W. J. Stein in a lecture entitled 'The Christ', as reported by Heather Farr: 'The Ritual of the Christian Community comes from Christ . . . Christ is alive in our own epoch as an Angel (of the Moon sphere). It was this Christ Angel which created the Christian Community Cultus. Rudolf Steiner spoke of this in private to Dr Rittelmeyer and myself.' At a lecture I asked her to give on behalf of the London Anthroposophists' group at Rudolf Steiner House in the 1980s, Evelyn Capel characterised the Renewal of the Mystery of Golgotha in the nineteenth century, which Rudolf Steiner first described in his London lecture of 2 May 1913, as a way to the resurrection of the Christ-consciousness in human beings on earth in the twentieth century, which underlies the movement for the renewal of Christianity in this century.

Close also to Evelyn's heart lay, in a way that remains true for her brave and loving successor at Temple Lodge, the special theme of Prester John and his relation to 'the unforgettable sky of Africa, with its regions of intensely alive air' (*Anthroposophical Quarterly*, Spring 1966).

From the eternal realms of the spirit, Evelyn Capel has lived a life of constant dedication to the Being of Christ and the community of those who would be with Him. To her I raise a thanking heart and trust in her and her future.

Jane Luxford
Pennine Community, Chapelthorpe, West Yorkshire, England

I believe I attended one of the first workshops on *The Philosophy of Spiritual Activity*. It has proved invaluable. By being guided through the book, in your amazing clear-thinking way, I was able to understand! This is a gift for life. I have drawn from its content in talks and daily life. Of all conferences, etc, that I have attended over the years this one is unsurpassed in the way I am able to make use of the content. I thank you for this.

Rhoda Mainstone
St Albans, Hertfordshire, England

I always enjoyed Evelyn's brisk, good-humoured retorts, either during a lecture, a discussion or in a personal conversation. I could smilingly agree with her instant, well-deserved and thoroughly good-natured put-downs.

When I retired from BBC Publications early in 1982 and was uncertain about my future, she encouraged me to 'help' Bert (her late husband) with the printing. For a month I tried (in vain) to master the machine while enjoying very much the friendly lunches and Bert's wonderful behind-the-scenes work that contributed so much to the high standards and meaningfulness of the Christian Community rituals.

Evelyn was one of the chief people who changed my life. Her clear mind and good sense helped me to see how I could grow in understanding, learn more about anthroposophy and 'live a normal life'. I was just about to get married for the first time in my late fifties to a recently widowed friend with a string of prestigious letters after his name (writer and lecturer) who 'believes through his eyes' but cannot attend to faltering descriptions of spiritual exotica!

I'll quote from old diaries some impressions of what Evelyn actually said, in which I still take delight:

A free action is a creative, good action per se. Influences that make it unfree are authority, religion, environment, parents, habit, reasoning.

Evelyn was being very positive about a free action being intuitive, not reasoned, and about the activity not the content of thinking putting you in touch with 'world ideas'.

You create in response to the situation itself – moral imagination – your *own* moral for that moment, freely grasped, created. We uniquely have purpose, respond to cause and effect. When bugged by shall I? shan't I? don't do either! *Create* rare and free action.

Joan Marcus
Stourbridge, West Midlands, England

I welcome the opportunity to say how greatly I appreciate Evelyn's books. At festival times I always turn to *The Christian Year* and find it a source of inspiration. My copy is full of sentences and paragraphs underlined and marked, which have particular meaning for me.

Her love of nature is beautifully described in the chapter on the Days of Resurrection, and the chapter on Ascension has such a depth of observation and delicacy of expression.

My father, Jack Bucknall, was a vicar in the Church of England. He was a socialist priest and an anthroposophist.* He and Evelyn had great stimulating conversations and father often remarked what a clear, good, penetrating mind she had – 'a fine intellect'. They got on very well – both strong and challenging people.

I last saw Evelyn when she came to Wales to celebrate the marriage of Anthony Matthews with his second wife, Sue. The service was held in a barn. The altar was bales of hay and the seats were bales of hay. My daughter Mary and I collected armfuls of wild flowers, which were in buckets each side of the altar.

Evelyn celebrated with such dignity and reverence it could just as well have been in a cathedral as in a barn.

* And in the forties and fifties he was involved in the then Fellowship of Ministers for the Study of Rudolf Steiner.

Ursula Marquardt
London, England

Evelyn had a large fount of knowledge, which she could convey to the uninitiated. I had problems understanding

Rudolf Steiner's *The Philosophy of Freedom*. Through Evelyn's interpretation I was able to understand it better.

She said: 'The Christian Community is a pioneering movement,' and she acted accordingly.

She was able to bring the living Christ to her listeners and readers, as well as the works of Rudolf Steiner.

Her books, too, are a great asset to me and, I presume, to other seekers too.

William Milne
Aberdeen, Scotland

My connection with The Christian Community goes back to the years just after the end of the Second World War. My father became interested on his return from the Burma Campaign in 1946. As a child, I attended the children's service in Aberdeen, which was held at 26 Carden Place, the home of The Christian Community at that time. I can well remember the excitement when Miss Evelyn Francis (as she then was) used to visit. My mother was very attached to the Scottish Episcopal Church, which she had attended as a child. She found her way into The Christian Community with some difficulty, but she always enjoyed the talks by Miss Francis. This was because Evelyn always spoke with authority and people felt secure in this.

My father went on a mission that Evelyn led to Germany in 1947 or 1948 to re-establish the links between The Christian Community in Britain and in Germany.

In the late sixties Evelyn came again to Aberdeen and gave talks about her trip to Africa, so I renewed my acquaintance with her. Then in 1975 I went to a summer conference taken by Evelyn, and I met for the first time her second husband, Bert Capel. We had a most enjoyable time at this conference, with Evelyn's fine talks and our relaxed trips into the lovely countryside. I noticed on this occasion her concern for other people. In Grasmere, the lady who ran one of the cafés had a daughter who was just about to have a child. Evelyn went back the next day to hear from the lady how her daughter was. Thus Evelyn showed a Christian

concern and interest in people outside her own congregation.

I have mentioned her splendid talks, which were based
on deep meditative study of the work of Rudolf Steiner. In
her ministry she also was an excellent pastor to those in
need. No one knows except Evelyn how many people she
has helped in distress or in crisis in their lives. Cecelia
Fisher, who was [honorary] treasurer at Temple Lodge for
many years, has some inkling of the scale of this work.

In the late seventies and early eighties my main contact
with Evelyn was at Eastertime at Temple Lodge. She always
held a conference over the Easter weekend, and I attended
this and often stayed on afterwards. It was always very inspiring to hear Evelyn talk on the mystery of the Easter
story, which she would unfold from Maundy Thursday to
Easter Sunday in a series of talks and sermons. Although
dealing with the same story, she always came at it from a
different angle. One year she would concentrate on the figure of Judas and the strange destiny in the betrayal. Another year she might concentrate on Pontius Pilate or
Doubting Thomas.

There was always an atmosphere of activity at Temple
Lodge, with talks, services, plays and hunting for eggs by
the children. Those Easter holidays will always be a very
special memory for me and, although I cannot remember in
detail the deep content that Evelyn gave over these week-
ends, I am sure that it goes on working within me.

Another stimulation to thought that Evelyn gave me was
the work on the twelve points of view. I have continued to
work with this over the years but have not got as far on as I
would have wished. Some years ago I shared some of
Evelyn's thoughts on this with my colleagues in the Aberdeen Waldorf school, and they also found it a stimulating
and interesting exercise.

It is as a speaker and teacher and writer of books that Evelyn
has influenced me most. I should also add that she was
above all else a friend – a friend who showed such interest
in my career and gave me encouragement in my work.

Evelyn's book on the parables, *The Timeless Storyteller*, has been much used by Waldorf teachers in their religion lesson. It is a masterpiece.

Dr Jacob Mirman and family
St Louis Park, Minnesota, USA

We are not members of the Anthroposophical Society or The Christian Community. Nevertheless, we had the pleasure of spending time with Evelyn Capel in 1991 when we stayed at Temple Lodge for several months. I had gone to London to study homoeopathy at the Royal London Homoeopathic Hospital and had brought with me my wife, Julia, and our two-year-old son, Nathan. Mrs Capel was very kind to let us stay at Temple Lodge for the duration of my course. Associating with her, as well as being able to participate in the activities of the Anthroposophical Society, including anthroposophical medicine seminars, served as a valuable step in our spiritual development.

Mrs Capel is a person of true wisdom and a deep understanding of the universal law. Her compassion for all people, regardless of their social standing or religious persuasion, was truly inspiring. A cleaning woman could relate to her just as easily as a visiting priest. She took people in and helped them realise their potential. She had inherent trust in the goodness of their intentions. She gave practical lessons in spirituality ever so gently and non-intrusively, so that the student would not even realise a lesson was given. Even now, six years later, we often remember Evelyn Capel as an example of how to live your life in this world.

Brid Montague
Belfast, Northern Ireland

I have found Evelyn a constant, sustaining source of practical, living wisdom always offered to fit capacity – and to suit the need. For instance, I can recall how a plan to consider Gerard Manley Hopkins could easily be set aside in the interests of other (perhaps unexpected) guests – although also with an explanation to myself. Her humorous, perceptive modes of working, with minimal fluency, could, I saw, accommodate most deaf and blind characteristics – with a huge grin thrown in for the genuinely physically deaf amongst us. I've delighted in her tenacious, imaginative innovations, proof that Christianity need not be dull.

From our first meeting, at a musical evening in the invitingly richly coloured, picture-filled Temple Lodge, I feel much indebted, and not only for unfailing hospitality. She has led the way in your country as woman and priest in a vibrant, inspiring manner. While it is difficult not to feel a little awestruck in such a presence, I have felt grateful and comforted by her undemanding sympathy and understanding, tolerant acceptance – especially at the time of Roger Biddulph's death.

Then, and subsequently in the Lake District, when some close associates of her own had just died, I caught glimpses of a deeply caring, accessible human being, herself vulnerable, yet with a tough job to do and perhaps, at times, precious little real understanding, support or help to do it. Is it too much to hope that Evelyn will come to feel the same understanding and love that she has herself so freely given?

I've just reread her article 'Looking back on a great adventure' [*The Threshing Floor* (May/June, 1989)]. This was written for the fiftieth anniversary of her priesthood, which I was happily able to attend. Once again I'm caught by the ironies and redeeming wit, also deeply moved by her early recognition of opportunities for kindness in deep suffering which do not lead to disempowerment. This was no bigoted patriot unable to find dignity in the other person's point of view.

The clarity and breadth of her thinking is an outstanding characteristic. I've got a long way to go before I begin to exhaust the readings made possible by her output. I can honestly say that I've appreciated everything to date. She should know already that I especially like her Easter plays. But I'm always drawn back to her beautifully constructed overview of the Holy Spirit at work. He who found the picture of the sparrow had the modern mind for the seventh century. It seems to me that Evelyn is one of those who has found the vantage point of the eagle. I have always particularly appreciated her invocation to the Holy Spirit (that much neglected personage) at the outset of discussion.

When last in London I was conveyed to the Royal Geographical Society. How could I fail to think of Evelyn, who herself had travelled so tirelessly? Later that day, as I took leave of London for Belfast, I found myself saying to her, as I disappeared into the Underground at Hammersmith:

> 'You take the high road
> And I'll take the low road.'

I'd much rather have invited her – as in the opening lines of another (Irish) poem – to 'come and dance with me in Ireland'. In Ireland she is as yet little known. In time I am hopeful that she will be recognised as an unsung pioneer – much in the mode of our indomitable, holy Brigid.

I had always hoped to bring Evelyn to Ireland but failed to find the right kind of opportunity. However, I have recently pursued a small opening by bringing her to the attention of a local lady professor at Queen's University, who makes no secret of her desire to accommodate priesthood for women.

Please give my warmest love to Evelyn. I imagine she's keeping her chin up – but I'd like to plant another kiss! May God bless and keep her always, may He fill her with overflowing happiness and peace.

Diane Mooney and family
Carshalton Beeches, Surrey, England

I am delighted to have the opportunity to write this tribute to Evelyn Capel on behalf of me and my family and to share it with others who have known and loved her for many years.

I first met Evelyn twenty-five years ago. I had become interested in Rudolf Steiner whilst attending an evening institute class in eurythmy under Jean Lynch. Although I still considered myself to be a Christian at that time, I had left the established church as it no longer made sense to me. I began reading anthroposophical books, mostly relating to children as my eldest daughter, Sarah, was then very young. A dear friend introduced me to Temple Lodge and Evelyn: I had found my spiritual home and the beginning of the most wonderful and exciting journey, with Evelyn as my guide and companion, sometimes directly but mostly through her sermons, lectures and books.

My husband, David, and I attended numerous children's services over the years with our three daughters, Sarah, Anna and Bella, all of whom were baptised by Evelyn, and Sarah and Anna were prepared for confirmation by her. The children's services provided a wealth of spiritual nourishment, through the services themselves and the activities that followed. We recall the plays written by Evelyn in which we all took part, country dancing in the garden, concerts, making turnip lanterns, the Easter egg hunt, jumping over the fire at St John's tide, the Advent spiral.

We remember with warmth and pleasure the spring conferences held at Woodford House, Keswick, run jointly by Evelyn and Ian and Angela Houston, where we visited stone circles, painted, sang, performed eurythmy, and listened to stimulating and enlightening talks by Evelyn, who seemed to have endless patience and energy for questions and observations. The healing landscape of the Lake District perfectly complemented the healing of the inner man provided by Evelyn and Ian. Those were golden days.

Celebrating the festivals at home has been a source of enjoyment, strength and insight for the family over the years, the inspiration for which has stemmed to a considerable extent from Evelyn's influence through the children's services, her poems, prayers and meditations.

Evelyn worked ceaselessly, with never-ending enthusiasm, to bring anthroposophy and The Christian Community to as many people as possible in as many parts of the world as possible. Yet she still found time to visit us at home when time permitted. She always encouraged the children and entertained us with amusing and interesting anecdotes from her vast repertoire of life experience.

I personally have struggled physically since my eldest daughter was born, the ramifications of which have made my life difficult and frustrating. I wonder how I would have survived and how I would have coped with the family without Evelyn and The Christian Community. So often her words and those of the Act of Consecration of Man have come to me at times of great need. Whilst writing this I have realised, for the first time, that Evelyn and Temple Lodge entered my life at just the right time. Evelyn's wisdom, knowledge, constancy, kindness and caring have supported and enlightened the Mooney family in a very special way, and we shall always treasure our memories and her books. She has sown so many seeds, and I am sure her influence will be felt through generations. Her gifts were manifold and awe-inspiring, but one of her special attributes was her willingness and ability to communicate with people of all ages from all walks of life. She is a true Christian, and she will always be a shining light to us. Our lives are indeed richer for knowing her and we owe her immense gratitude.

Muriel Napper
Reigate, Surrey, England

I should like to thank Evelyn for the services of The Christian Community that I attended at Temple Lodge for some years and that meant much to me. Also for the private talks we had on several occasions and the help from these that has ensued.

Many books by Evelyn and other authors have been brought before the public through Temple Lodge Publishing, which Evelyn was instrumental in founding.

Maria Nimmo
Oban, Argyll, Scotland

When I look back I realise that it was a relatively short period during which I came to The Christian Community worship in Glenilla Road, where there was a chapel. At that time, in 1946, I was doing social work in Bethnal Green, London, and it was quite an effort to get to Glenilla Road – my weekly wage being £5. I loved the service and the inspiration from it.

In 1948 I married a Scotsman, and when I told Evelyn that I would not be coming to the service and why, she wanted to know where I was going to live. She then told me that her half-sister Win Crawford was living in Oban, where her husband was the surgeon at the hospital. Evelyn wrote to her sister about me coming to live in Oban and that I would not know anyone. The result was that, once I got to Oban, I had a visit from Win, and we were firm friends from then on until Win's death in 1980.

During the seventies Evelyn came to a conference on Iona, which both my husband and I attended, and where she was one of the three contributors. Win brought her, if I remember correctly, and both stayed with me. I also went with Evelyn's groups to Israel and 'In the Steps of St Paul'. Both trips were an inspiration.

I grew up in a manse (my father was a Lutheran pastor), and I have searched for strength to cope with life's challenges. I feel that I have never been near enough to any anthroposophical centre to really participate, but I would say that Evelyn's writings helped to enlarge my vision and throw light on aspects that I did not quite understand in the Bible.

Mollie Padday
Jordans, Buckinghamshire, England

I am happy to respond to your request, even although my knowledge of Evelyn is really fragmentary. We met at the time of Lady Dorothy Pratt's last few months, when I was trying to help by going along with Dorothy's great wish – to be able to remain at home until the end of her life. Together we achieved this and during the course of it Revd Evelyn came to visit her. It was a long way for Evelyn to come but her visits were exceptional and always left Dorothy 'up-lifted'.

I have two special personal memories of Evelyn. One day, after Dorothy had died, she came because there were some items left to Evelyn and she came to collect them. She brought with her a young lad of about ten years old. It must have been a special day out for this lad, and a chance to see the country, since Dorothy lived in Prestwood in Bucking-hamshire. I was told that this lad was becoming good at French and Evelyn was insisting that he should not use a dictionary to look up French words. I wondered at this and thought it over many times. Eventually I thought that, like the second story I shall relate, it was to do with the fact that Evelyn is so positive. I think she felt there was a better way of learning new words other than by getting bogged down in a dictionary.

The second occasion was a further visit to collect articles. This time Evelyn brought a young man recently released from prison. She was urging him to set up his own kitchen at Hammersmith in order to begin to make a small living from cooking. We found all sorts of small things that would help him, and again I was amazed by Evelyn's imagination and positive approach through the simplest of things, and her obvious steady guidance that seemed to me to be as strong as an oak tree.

For me, two lovely occasions that I remember vividly.

Cynthia Parker
Blackburn, Victoria, Australia

As a young girl growing up in the sheltered colonial and patriarchal background of Zimbabwe, then Southern Rho-desia, in the sixties, I first met Evelyn as the twelve-year-old daughter of a woman who had recently embraced anthro-posophy and The Christian Community (Mrs K. M. Antho-ny, my mother). Evelyn was one of the most regular and pi-oneering of the overseas visitors who arrived to nurture the beginnings of spiritual science in that part of the world. The ongoing nature and commitment of her visits was one of the aspects that forged my connection with Evelyn. The way she acknowledged and treated the black people with a human respect that was uncustomary in my upbringing was an influential window to another perspective on life. It gave me respect for my own repressed dark unconscious.

Another major influence was my baptism and confirmation. At twelve years of age I was baptised with my older brother into The Christian Community in the lounge room of our home and, ever able to overcome obstacles, two years later Evelyn arranged for me to travel on my own by air to Pretoria in South Africa where I joined the confirmation class that she conducted that year, 1965. The deep religious significance of these events took another thirty-three years to unfold, while the immediate significance of the experience was one of the joy, liberation and expansiveness of a sheltered young girl encountering the wider world.

Then began for me a deep and intense dedication to anthroposophy and, as a teacher, to Waldorf education. During these years I visited Evelyn only once, at the age of twenty, when I stayed at Temple Lodge for a short time. She suggested appropriate things for me to do in London, which included a visit to the Tate Gallery and a performance of *Abelard and Héloise*, whose nude scenes both shocked the sheltered colonial girl and at the same time spoke of the possibility of a broader tolerance of, and open-mindedness to, the world, through Evelyn's attitudes. This was a further important subliminal influence on my outer development.

During the next twenty-five years – a journey through the trials of split thinking, feeling and willing towards the reintegration of these faculties under the guidance of the higher self – a journey began in South Africa and continued in Australia. During these years Evelyn was only an aerogramme away, and on several occasions she encouraged me with an astuteness and vision that went beyond the parameters of my circumstantial difficulties. I believe it to have been an expression of her knowledge of, and her faith in, my individual spirit and its destiny, stemming from those connections forged in the early times around the sacraments of baptism and confirmation. Out of so few and such brief encounters grew so much. Evelyn stimulated my growth and development in two directions – both in my inner life and in its outward expression.

To this extent, namely, that thirty-three years after my baptism I have been able to renew my connection to The Christian Community now in Melbourne, Australia, having emerged from what in some respects was a sojourn in subterranean depths, an underground stream of life that now bubbles up to the earth's surface and seeks a new direction, strongly connected to the life of the Christ Spirit.

For all this I can be grateful to, not only or mainly Evelyn Capel, but to other seen and unseen influences as well, but here we can particularly highlight Evelyn's contribution, which in essence seems to have had the potency of a homoeopathic healing medicine.

One might sound trite in voicing the wish to at least experience once in life the joys and rewards of influencing another on the journey of the spirit, as Evelyn no doubt has done for so many. In writing this, I'm sure we all renew our connection with her for the rest of this earthly life of hers and on into the next.

Pat Pears
Penicuik, Midlothian, Scotland

Anyone who did not know Evelyn would wonder – is she male or female? Especially as, when in the army, she was a colonel. I love her dearly and always will. She helped by just being such a fund of sure knowledge and always willing to listen.

Dorothy Percival
St Albans, Hertfordshire, England

Long before meeting The Christian Community or anthroposophy, I lived in Queen Caroline Street, opposite Temple

Lodge. I would often dream of the (then) blue door in the wall leading through to Temple Lodge, but with a demanding job interpreting for visiting overseas doctors, I ignored these promptings!

Years later, when I'd found anthroposophy and moved away from London, I felt the need for ritual in my spiritual life and sought out Evelyn – through her publications at first. The clarity and authority of *Seven Sacraments in The Christian Community* struck me immediately, and I felt an immediate point of contact with this fellow Oxford woman graduate. Her academic credibility was an added pleasure for me, as many Steiner-inspired authors lack Evelyn's crispness and command of syntax. As soon as I'd read it, *Seven Sacraments in The Christian Community* inspired me to seek out the Act of Consecration, and I knew it was absolutely what I needed within moments of attending my first service at Temple Lodge. Thank you, Evelyn!

Since then, I've bought everything Evelyn's written and greatly been enriched in my family and spiritual life. In particular, *Death: The End is the Beginning* has been of great value in coping with bereavements and in my relationship to the dead, particularly in the difficult first few days. Had I not read it many years beforehand, I'd have found my parents' deaths, within a few months of one another, very much harder to cope with. In fact, I discover that I have three copies by my bedside!

The Tenth Hierarchy and *Reincarnation within Christianity* are the two other particularly valuable books of Evelyn's that I must also mention. Whole worlds of difficult content are presented clearly and concisely – no mean feat, and one that makes great use of the historian's skills as well as the priest's.

The first meeting I had with Evelyn is the one that remains most strongly etched in my memory. This energetic, poised, rather intense and fiercely intelligent lady had a pair of the brightest, most piercing eyes I'd every seen – alert, kindly, enquiring, yet with a deeply impish twinkle!

Johan Henri Quanjer
New Humanity Journal, London, England

I remember how extremely well Evelyn Capel researched her talks and how definite she was in her views. It was a joy to listen to her. She stimulated thought processes in my mind, which I found most evocative. It was obvious that Sir George Trevelyan and Evelyn were beautifully integrated as speakers on the same platform, with Sir George adding a touch of poetry to the proceedings.

Dear Evelyn's thinking and presence made a great impact on me, and no doubt she has left her imprint on the mindsphere (or cosmic internet)! This is a brilliant legacy for future generations to benefit from. She – as I understand it – lived to enrich society and succeeded.

Please do give her my blessings. From what I remember she was very kind to me. This I appreciated immensely.

It is all part of an era that is now passing away, but the great good Evelyn's generation did will be remembered and continued by those who follow. Nothing of great worth is ever lost and can be 'accessed' and utilised in ways most suitable for a new era.

I am pleased you contacted me, allowing me to cast my mind back, which can be most salutary.

Claire Rauter
London, England

I have known Evelyn since our return from Scotland in 1947/48. In the summer of 1948 she baptised our son – the first christening to be held in the new church at Glenilla Road.

For me she epitomised the brilliant and beautiful Englishwoman of learning and in my memory her many hats played quite an important part!

No surprise that she produced in her colleagues feelings of utter despair as well as admiration through the years. For so many families – including ours – her loving concern dominated, as did her humour.

Elizabeth Storr
Heerenveen, Netherlands

I have been always very pleased and grateful to have spent some time in Temple Lodge. To have known Revd Evelyn Capel was the most wonderful time. My destiny changed for the rest of my life, for the best. I helped Revd Evelyn Capel with everything. We got on very well, and one day she presented me with her book *The Reappearing of Christ*, signed 'Temple Lodge, St John's Tide 1983, with warm thanks and loving wishes from the author'!

Yes, I miss everything, but I never forget, and my loving thoughts will always be with Revd Evelyn Capel.

Hazel Straker
Coleg Elidyr, Rhandirmwyn, Carmarthenshire, Wales

In her capacity as a priest of The Christian Community Evelyn has done much in her life, through her many books, lectures, sermons and personal conversations, to present spiritual truths in a way understandable to people with very varied backgrounds. Her personal conviction of spiritual realities made what she brought acceptable even to those who find it hard to recognise spiritual facts. However, her personal convictions being very strong did not always make her life easy. Her work with her congregation was very lively, and she created a rich cultural life that included many artistic activities.

I came to know Evelyn in 1948 at Albrighton Hall, a conference house of The Christian Community near Shrewsbury, where I was for a time a member of the 'crew' who looked after the house. The priests held their synods there, and Evelyn came to these. At the close of their serious considerations, the priests would present a social evening, full of humour, to thank the 'crew' for looking after them, and that enabled us also to get to know them.

Evelyn was a great supporter of Willi Sucher and his star work, *Astrosophy*. She would regularly invite him to lecture at Temple Lodge, the Christian Community centre in West

London where she worked, holding services and bringing about the rich cultural life already mentioned. As a driver, I accompanied Willi Sucher and his wife and always enjoyed the warm atmosphere of the house. After the lecture we would sit around the kitchen table for refreshments and lively conversation.

I have a very vivid memory of the memorial Act of Consecration that Evelyn held for Willi Sucher in Stroud, 1985. It was a truly festive event, which Evelyn introduced by a very moving sermon of appreciation of his life and work.

Evelyn has contributed much both to The Christian Community and anthroposophy. I am grateful to have known her and to be able to write an appreciation to join those of many others.

Ann Thomas
Bowerchalke, Wiltshire, England

My husband and I have been anthroposophists since attending a two-week course – 'Towards a New Social Order' – at Emerson College fourteen years ago. We were fortunate enough to have both Francis Edmunds and John Davy giving lectures. As a result of that course, we both trained as Steiner teachers at Rudolf Steiner House. On occasions, while training, it was necessary to stay in London overnight. We decided to attend the Act of Consecration of Man at Temple Lodge. We had no idea what to expect. We met Evelyn then for the first time.

After the celebration, Evelyn spoke to us with great warmth and invited us to a shared lunch round the large table at Temple Lodge. From that date we attended services as often as possible at Temple Lodge and participated in courses and events when we were able. Evelyn has a good combination of Martha and Mary in her make-up, and in her welcome and lack of superiority she reminds me of the reception one receives on attending a function at a Baptist church. One of our daughters is a Baptist and when we visit we attend the church.

When, twelve years ago, a close relative endured a harsh tragedy it was, after some years, to Evelyn that I eventually went, uncertain whether I would be chastised, advised or dismissed. I have never before experienced such sensitive, unsentimental perception or received such sound advice and support.

In Evelyn's writing I find what I have been searching for and travelling towards all my life. The vocabulary itself contains such a healing quality. The profundity of her writing comes to life in one's mind. Through Evelyn I have been led to a far deeper understanding of the Resurrection.

Evelyn's learning and study astound me. She must have had to practise much self-denial and self-control to achieve this, and yet she is not proud and unattainable – just firm and unwavering. This intellectuality has been so wonderfully metamorphosed into deep, imaginative, wise and healing words. She shows much compassion and patience with those who are searching and stumbling and is never patronising.

If I were to be banished to a desert island for a while and could take one possession with me, it would be the books written by Evelyn Capel. Top of the list would be *The Christian Year*, *The Reappearing of Christ*, *The Tenth Hierarchy*, *The Timeless Storyteller*, *Christ in the Old and New Testaments*, *Studies in Christian Meditation* and *An Introduction to Counselling*.

Olive and Jim Twamley

Faversham, Kent, England (Jim Twamley is a former trustee of The Christian Community/London West)

We were introduced to Evelyn through the cremation service of Dr Raeside in June 1972; Evelyn officiated. From then on we were closely associated with Temple Lodge, becoming members of The Christian Community, and Jim was a trustee for some years.

While we were there Evelyn ran a philosophy course for Hammersmith Technical College, which was attended by local folk. She also invited professional musicians, artists and exponents of many other disciplines to Temple Lodge. Her breadth of knowledge was always awe-inspiring.

We well remember many holidays abroad, which she personally organised down to the minutest detail. She had many contacts in foreign parts, all making us very welcome on her behalf. Incidentally, she usually wore a large red hat on these holidays so that her group could pick her out in a crowd.

Numerous people sought her advice and support, which she freely gave. She had an amazing ability to get to the heart of a problem. We still have friends who relate to us how Evelyn gave them fresh insight into their difficulties, which changed the course of their lives for good.

We wish Evelyn a long period of rest from her physical activities and think of her often.

Gabriele Weber

Berlin, Germany (translation coordinated by the editor)

In 1970 Michael Heidenreich took the Berlin Youth Circle on a camping holiday through England and Scotland. On the way back we stayed at Woodford House in Keswick, the conference centre of The Christian Community in Britain. I decided to offer my services as a waitress for the 1971 season after my Abitur examinations.

Among others, there was an important Whitsun conference to which Evelyn Capel came. She immediately befriended me, and I was able to join in a walk that self-same evening. The impression Mrs Capel made reminded me of Helen Keller whom, of course, I knew only from a book. There was a positive atmosphere around her. I would describe Evelyn Capel as friendly, accepting, modest but self-confident, self-respecting and upright, inside and out.

On returning home at the end of the season, I stopped over at Temple Lodge (popularly referred to as 'Capel Lodge'!). Thus, on 29 September 1971 I was able to renew my acquaintance with Mr and Mrs Capel, who made me very welcome and offered me a lovely evening dinner, their joint effort. House and garden were beautifully kept.

I am grateful to have been able to meet Evelyn Capel and send her warm-hearted greetings.

Dr Basil Williams
Chrysalis, Arlington, Massachusetts, USA

I first met Evelyn Capel when she came to Harlemville, New York, in the spring of 1987. She lectured on the four archangels. I was greatly impressed with her sincerity and with her spiritual knowledge about the archangels and the whole company of heaven. She gave such a living picture that was so real for me. After her lecture I spoke to her concerning her spiritual insights. I then decided to study with her in England when I visited the anthroposophical physicians in London. I spent two months at Temple Lodge. When I was not involved with my anthroposophical studies I would have conferences with her. I had many questions, which she helped me to understand better through discussion or directed study. One of the statements she made then that I feel is coming to reality at this time is: 'Everyone will cross the threshold by the year 2000, whether or not he or she is spiritually prepared.'

After 1987 I would visit Evelyn periodically at Temple Lodge, just as a student would consult a teacher. She always had the time, and she welcomed my visits. I felt she was not only a spiritual teacher but also a friend. She was interested in every person who sought her help. She was very proud of her education from Oxford. This education gave her depth and credibility as an educator and as a scholar. With over fifty years' work as a woman priest she was an exceptional personality with wisdom of life's experiences. She truly lived life on the earth and extended her spiritual knowledge to those who came to her for counsel. She had some difficulties with different individuals, but I really did not experience this with Evelyn. Perhaps it was because of my understanding and appreciation of the English folk soul, but this is not completely the main reason. I was truly fond of Evelyn and had love for this personality, perhaps like a son, that transcended the usual misunderstandings that can occur between people.

I was impressed first with her as an individual who well represented the consciousness soul. She was so much the individual who worked and believed with conviction in the spiritual and she did not deviate from this. One was always prepared for the truth from Evelyn, and I never expected anything different. Secondly, she was every bit a priest. She was the best of priests in my mind. Her sermons were magnificent, very deep in spiritual content and yet applicable to daily life. One Sunday I was deeply moved by her profound sermon. As she left the podium, she had the practical state of mind to turn down the heat. This was Evelyn. She could discuss with deep devotion spiritual matters at one moment and take care of necessary earthly matters as they arose. Her counsel and advice went out to all equally, the rich and poor, the educated and the uneducated. I believe she had a true Christian love for those she interacted with, and she took the time and interest for all.

My wife, Christina, and I travelled extensively throughout Britain to many of the mystery centres with Evelyn. We reaped rich rewards and knowledge because of her understanding of anthroposophy and Christian history. After one Sunday service, the congregation visited the Henry VIII mound near London. As we approached this old Celtic mound, Evelyn said, 'We must approach the top by this specific path because it is right and proper, just as the old Celts did in the past.' She had some inner insight that was so definite and real, almost as if in some previous time she had been there.

We often studied Rudolf Steiner's pastoral medicine course, together with other physicians and priests. These were very informative studies for me, as an anthroposophical physician. With a humorous note, I once said to Evelyn, 'In our next life I will be the priest and you will be the physician . . .' She retorted, 'And I will make a very good physician . . .'

Evelyn was always a passionate promoter of anthroposophy and she was extremely well read in the anthroposophical literature. She included her insights in her own writings. In America it is unusual to find a person who has not read one of her many books on anthroposophy or The Christian Community. In her actions and in her words she wished to enliven anthroposophy and The Christian Community with the arts. Christina and I often reminisce about the delightful conference at Lattendales [Friends' Fellowship of Healing] with members of The Christian Community. Evelyn helped organise the event so that Ian Houston, pianist and artist, along with his wife, Angela, could bring the dimension of music and colour to the study. While giving a workshop on *The Philosophy of Spiritual Activity* in our home in Harlemville, Evelyn asked to include lyre playing, singing and eurythmy with the process of studying Steiner's important book.

It was a golden age for us and the delightful days spent with Evelyn will not be forgotten. Our lives have been enriched and spiritually nurtured by her presence. She had a big heart, and she generously shared her feelings and love with all of us. I consider myself fortunate to have known Evelyn, and I truly appreciate the many happy moments that we have spent with this truly unique personality in this lifetime.

Christina Williams
Arlington, Massachusetts, USA

Evelyn came into my life through her books during my Waldorf Early Childhood teacher training programme in Detroit, Michigan. I discovered *The Christian Year*. It provided a rich and true backdrop for the festival work in the classroom. Now, some twenty years later, I am still using the book and highly recommending it to other teachers and parents. But it was her book *The Mystery of Growing Up: Childhood and the Spiritual Life: Practical Ideas for Parents and Teachers* that awakened in me yet another reason for wanting to meet Evelyn in person.

At the time I was coming into the Waldorf training course, I was simultaneously working on a master's degree in English at the university. My topic was a seventeenth-century mystic, poet and clergyman, Thomas Traherne. He was not well known or well documented in academic circles so I rarely found anyone who could relate to my interest in this writer. What a happy surprise I had when Evelyn quoted this poet of joy throughout her book. Here, in Evelyn, was a priest, anthroposophist and literary scholar. I fancied that one day I would travel to England to meet her.

But karma had another pattern, because Evelyn came to America in 1987. Just one week after moving from Michigan to the New York/Massachusetts area, I saw a small notice that Evelyn Capel was visiting friends and having morning sessions about the Sermon on the Mount. I attended the sessions. It was the beginning of a treasured friendship.

My husband, Basil, and I visited Britain many times to be with Evelyn, travel with her and be guided by her through subtle and not so subtle questions about life, anthroposophy, Christianity. We watched her relate to various people in her English circle. Sometimes she was firm, even blunt, demanding, but mostly we perceived her absolute kindliness and compassion, especially for the 'fringe' people who found their way to her Temple Lodge haven – the poor, misshapen, addicted, misguided were given opportunities by Evelyn to turn their lives around. This was done without sentimentality but with clarity and matter-of-factness.

She found time for people – no place was too far for her to travel to help bring Christianity in word and deed. Her trips to the outskirts of Wales for religious classes for poor, struggling families were amazing. She performed a wedding and a baptism under trying conditions there but was never daunted by the outer discomforts.

Evelyn could walk through muddy terrains but she could also weave light-filled thoughts with the precision of a scholar. At times I would ask a question about a passage in the Bible or about a given statement in a Steiner lecture. She eagerly took the time to pursue the ramifications of the question – giving at first an overview and then saying, 'To-morrow we'll talk further.' The next day she came forth with examples, and even stories, to answer the question even more fully.

Evelyn's grasp of anthroposophy and of *The Philosophy of Spiritual Activity* has been a true inspiration for me. She has made the ideas her own, giving them the warmth of her own life experiences.

Several times we had Evelyn visit our home in Harlemville, New York. One week she gave a workshop on her book *Towards Freedom: A Journal of Discovery through Rudolf Steiner's 'The Philosophy of Spiritual Activity'*. It shows how she has worked through the ideas – clarity and warmth throughout. One moment in the workshop has had a special meaning for me. We had been working through questions of freedom, moral imagination, intuition. She then brought forth an example from her own life studies of the Bible. She spoke of the need for community when creative thinking has beheld the same idea, even if the mental pictures are different. She wove in the vision of New Jerusalem as a picture of community. She reminded us of the picture of the Last Supper, of John in the position of listening to what the heart of Christ was saying. She reminded us how important listening was, to leave a space so that freedom can be inspired. Each human has the work of how to receive the inspiration from the spiritual world and then how to keep it. The latter is what we do for each other in communities. We help each other keep the inspiration – a Whitsun image really – one heart, one mind.

I am filled with gratitude for what Evelyn brought through her life experiences as an anthroposophist and as a priest.

One of my last travels with Evelyn was to Dornach for the English week of the Mystery Plays. All the insights and sharing have a place in my memory but I want to tell you of one encounter that speaks to Evelyn's astuteness, compassion and objectivity. Janet (Evelyn's sister), Evelyn and I were having lunch at the Speisehaus. We were deep in conversation about the conference. Nearby a young retarded woman sat down, clutching a hand-knitted doll. I had a passing thought of how one would acknowledge someone who doesn't have the usual social skills to interact. It was a question I pondered. Evelyn didn't seem to notice the girl at all. But when we stood up to leave Evelyn held back a bit, took a few steps to the girl's table and made a comment, showed a genuine interest in the knitted doll, and a brief encounter via the doll took place. This was an act of recognition that went beyond words. That brief meeting between the true priest and the lonely soul continues to shine as a picture of Evelyn's gift to the world beyond all the obvious talents.

Evelyn's interest in others brings me to a poet that she quoted during a retreat at Lattendales when we were talking about the Etheric Christ. I met Evelyn on the wings of the seventeenth-century poet Thomas Traherne who starts the poem 'Wonder' with 'How like an angel came I down . . .' At Lattendales, Evelyn took me beyond wings to the air itself with Stevie Smith's poem 'The Airy Christ' [from *The Collected Poems of Stevie Smith*, published by Allen Lane 1975, reproduced by kind permission]:

After reading Dr Rieu's translation of St Mark's Gospel.

'Who is this that comes in splendour, coming from the blaz-
  ing East?
This is he we had not thought of, this is he the airy Christ.

Airy, in an airy manner in an airy parkland walking,
Others take him by the hand, lead him, do the talking.

But the Form, the airy One, frowns an airy frown,
What they say he knows must be, but he looks aloofly
  down,

Looks aloofly at his feet, looks aloofly at his hands,
Knows they must, as prophets say, nailèd be to wooden
  bands.

As he knows the words he sings, that he sings so happily
Must be changed to working laws, yet sings he ceaselessly.

Those who truly hear the voice, the words, the happy song,
Never shall need working laws to keep from doing wrong.

Deaf men will pretend sometimes they hear the song, the
    words,
And make excuse to sin extremely; this will be absurd.

Heed it not. Whatever foolish men may do the song is cried
For those who hear, and the sweet singer does not care that
    he was crucified.

For he does not wish that men should love him more than
    anything
Because he died; he only wishes they would hear him sing.'

My heart is filled with gratitude for coming to know
Evelyn Capel.

Nicholas Woollven
London, England (secretary, The Benen Trust)

My first – albeit very faint – memory of Evelyn concerns my
own christening at Glenilla Road, at which Stanley Drake
was also present. Then there was Benen House at Draycott
Place, Chelsea, in the mid-fifties, which may, among other
things, explain my abiding attachment to basements. This
continued when I began to go regularly to Temple Lodge in
the mid-sixties and, among many others, experienced the
strong camaraderie of the informal Sunday lunches in the
basement, presided over by Evelyn's sisters, Janet and
Edith.

Whilst these congenial lunches greatly advanced the social role of The Christian Community, no one who has ever
met and known Evelyn could possibly doubt her serious-
ness of purpose and her overriding aims of furthering the
importance and understanding of the Act of Consecration

of Man and the world importance of the teachings of Rudolf Steiner.

Looking back now, I marvel at Evelyn's importance as a pioneer in both these complementary realms and her indefatigable pursuit of these aims.

Whilst the central importance of the sacraments was tirelessly advocated, she also did everything she could to foster artistic activities, educational activities (in the broadest sense) and – long before it became fashionable amongst other churches (and gained unfortunate brand names like 'Outreach') – to make genuine progress in evolving a dialogue with other churches and spiritual movements of all kinds.

In this crusade, her development of Temple Lodge came to embrace a rich variety of practical artistic work (including painting classes and drama), exhibitions, concerts (which helped to launch such now-famous ensembles as Capricorn) and ILEA evening classes in music appreciation and other subjects, including Evelyn's own psychology classes. This led to a very helpful working relationship with the local authorities in Hammersmith.

Evelyn has also been a steadfast promoter of conferences, whether at Temple Lodge on *The Philosophy of Spiritual Activity* and in joint ventures with Sir George Trevelyan of The Wrekin Trust, or at The Christian Community's Woodford House at Keswick. There, following the Act of Consecration of Man, the days would be filled with music, painting, walking and discussions.

Evelyn was also very active in pastoral care and helped a great many people, and not just members of The Christian Community, with their own particular personal problems. One such person was the now world-famous David Helfgott, who stayed with his wife at Temple Lodge on several occasions. He used to play 'special requests' for my aunt – Cecelia Fisher – whilst she worked in the afternoons bringing the congregation's accounts up to date! (What a pity that Evelyn and Temple Lodge get only one slightly misleading reference in his wife's recently published account of his life.)

Evelyn was also always very active in organising members' excursions overseas to the Goetheanum and the Holy Land (several times to both) and to Christian Communities in continental Europe, including most notably, as I remember, to our beleaguered friends in the Eastern Bloc. Indeed Evelyn showed no dread of communist bureaucracy or tinpot officialdom of any kind! I remember that she took a close personal interest in priests in Czechoslovakia and Russia whose fulfilment of their religious responsibilities was hampered at that time, and I well remember a tense but exhilarating twenty-four hours in Prague whilst our small party lent moral support by its very presence. It was subsequently very rewarding when priests from the East were enabled to come and celebrate in Temple Lodge.

Evelyn's importance as an international ambassador for The Christian Community cannot be underestimated, as the volume of contributions to this memoir will surely demonstrate. It was a most significant step when – with Bert Capel's practical help – the Temple Lodge Press (now Temple Lodge Publishing) was established. This has, in particular, enabled the publication or reissue of a number of important works from Christian Community members and anthroposophists in other parts of the world, including Russia.

Evelyn has given more than just a normal working life in continual support of The Christian Community both at home and abroad. I would like to believe that the Community shall see her like again. Fortunately – although she is now in retirement from the priesthood – her wisdom and clear-sighted practical advice will be of enduring value to all through her many books. Long may they remain in print!

Evelyn Francis Capel (photo: William Bishop).

Chronology and Profile

Some brief notes on early days (in the UK) of The Christian Community – a movement for religious renewal founded in 1922 – and on the life history of Evelyn Francis Capel.

Dr Alfred Heidenreich, a founding priest of the Community and its first leader in the UK, came to England in 1929 with his wife, Marta Heimeran. They lived at The Attic, 64 Avenue Road, Highgate, then retired with friends to a bungalow at Lancing, Sussex, to work undisturbed on the English version of the sacramental texts and to celebrate the first Act of Consecration of Man on British soil.

By 1931, 1001 Finchley Road, a semi-detached two-storey house near Golders Green known as '1001', had become the Community's London headquarters. In 1936, as the congregation grew and needed a larger chapel, the Community rented (on a short lease) The Studio at No. 7 Maitland Park Villas, Chalk Farm, now obliterated by a council estate. (As a priest, Dr Heidenreich was allowed to stay in England during the Second World War.)

In 1944 The Community bought 34 Glenilla Road, Belsize Park, and named it The Social Centre. The Community's journal records that Evelyn was in charge of the Centre and that it had been acquired through a truly extraordinary sequence of events following upon a hint taken up by her. It had an adjoining plot (No. 32), which was licensed for building but was at the time used as a tennis court. In 1948 a 'temporary' church was built on this site, eventually acquiring permanent status from the local authority. (The lease on The Studio had by then expired.)

In 1946, The Community acquired Albrighton Hall (a Jacobean manor house near Shrewsbury, Shropshire) as a conference centre/guest house. Two years later this replaced '1001' as the Community's headquarters and Dr Heidenreich's base.

It was sold in 1953, having become 'too big and top-heavy', and the Community acquired the smaller Woodford House (a Victorian boarding house near Keswick, Cumbria). Dr Heidenreich found this change 'painful' and moved to Glenilla Road, which then became the Community's headquarters. It appears that this is when Evelyn branched out on her own, apparently never drawing a stipend, rather than leave London to found another Community centre as she had been requested to do. (She had held the fort at Glenilla Road for seven years during and after the war, as Community secretary, ratepayer and trustee.)

Evelyn Francis Capel

1911   Born 23 March in Stow-on-the-Wold in the Cotswold Hills. She was one of five sisters in a Nonconformist family and, after the early death of her father, grew up in Cheltenham, Gloucestershire.

1925–29   Pate's Grammar School for Girls, Cheltenham (now a co-educational school)
Oxford School Certificate (first in all England)
Oxford & Cambridge Higher School Certificate
State scholarship and county leaving scholarship to:

1929–32   Somerville College, Oxford (non-denominational, with a strong tradition of Nonconformity)
Hons. Modern History, Class II
Discovers, in this cosmopolitan atmosphere, that she is a natural vegetarian, despite having been brought up to eat meat.

1932–36   One of the first management trainees at J. Lyons & Co., Hammersmith, London (the famous caterers and food-manufacturing business – then a family firm run by the Salmon and Gluckstein families).
A friend introduces her to anthroposophy and The Christian Community; she starts writing for the Community journal and visits the 1935 international summer conference in Berlin.

1936–39   Trains at the Christian Community Seminary, Stuttgart, after a crash course in Germany to learn the language.

1939   Ordained on 18 June in London. Returns to Germany for a few months, catching one of the last trains to Holland before the declaration of the Second World War, then a plane to England.

1939–44   There is a wartime policy to concentrate all Community priests at '1001', from where they visit scattered groups all over the country.

1944–51   Evelyn is placed in charge of The Community's Social Centre at 34 Glenilla Road – the church is built in 1948. During this period she is resident priest for a few months at Albrighton Hall, then travels as The Community's ambassador overseas because Dr Heidenreich, still a German citizen, is not allowed to do so.

1945   Represents the Community in Holland at the ordination of the first Dutch woman priest.

1946   Visits the congregations of The Christian Community in Germany (British and American zones) to encourage the rebuilding of their groups and churches. Travels (with the rank of Colonel) under the auspices of the Religious Affairs Department of the Allied Control Commission for Germany.

1947   Similar visits to Czechoslovakia and Austria, with a stopover in Switzerland

1951   Dr Heidenreich settles at Glenilla Road and expects Evelyn to set up a Community centre outside London (probably Bristol). She marries Samuel Derry, then sets out on her own, not wishing to leave London.

1951–54 Operates from various temporary addresses; the congregation starts to call itself 'London West'.

1954–61 As a stopgap, Colonel and Mrs Innes – she was a Community member – offer London West the use of three floors of their huge six-storey 1890s house at 34 Draycott Place, Chelsea (now a hotel).

1960   The untimely death (from cancer) of her first husband, Samuel Derry

1961   With the help of private loans and donations, London West acquires Temple Lodge, a Georgian house at 51 Queen Caroline Street, Hammersmith, to which a studio was added by the artist, Sir Frank Brangwyn, in the early 1900s. Two independent trusts are formed to cover purchase and administration.

1967   Marries second husband, Bert Capel.

1972–84 The main part of Temple Lodge becomes too small for current activities. The Brangwyn studio (previously leased out) is reconstructed to form a new chapel, a restaurant, and useful space for a number of purposes. Extra sleeping accommodation is provided in the old house and beehives are installed in the garden.

1970s   The local Addison Adult Education Institute uses Temple Lodge as one of its outposts. This is just one part of Evelyn's thirty-four years of conferences, lectures, discussions, and creative activities at the Lodge and further afield.

1986   The untimely death (from heart failure) of second husband, Bert Capel.

1989   Celebration of fifty years in the priesthood.

1990   Temple Lodge Publishing is set up as a separate venture, after a series of in-house printing/publishing efforts during the 1980s.

1991   Fellowship of the Royal Society of Arts (to which Evelyn was introduced by Dame Diana Reader Harris).

1991   Various schemes (during the 1980s) culminate in the Barbara Manteuffel/Stuart Page design for a freestanding church at the bottom of the Temple Lodge garden. (This has now been shelved, but hopefully may arise elsewhere, as a national project.)

During thirty-four years at Temple Lodge (1961–1995) Evelyn journeyed overseas to build up congregations, encourage individuals and administer the sacraments. (In 1965 The Community's journal praised her enthusiasm and the solid preparation that led to the foundation of a Christian Community in South Africa. And Evelyn led several groups to Prague to express support for The Christian Community, which lived on during both Nazi and communist oppression.) All these journeys are too numerous to list here, as are the many UK and overseas trips organised for the congregation, often in the faithful Temple Lodge minibus.

At both Benen House and Temple Lodge, Evelyn was fully committed to the preaching, teaching, celebration of sacraments, and pastoral work of The Christian Community. Her 'mission statement' (as printed in Temple Lodge's own magazine during the 1980s) was: 'The Christian Community is a Church born in the present century among contemporary people who long for a living faith and understanding of Christianity. Its purpose is that within it shall be celebrated the seven sacraments in their renewed form, that the souls and destinies of men and women shall find healing, and that Christian truth shall be understood anew.'

1996   Evelyn retires to the Raphael Medical Centre, Hildenborough, near Tonbridge, Kent, after a lifetime of devoted service to The Christian Community.

This chronology will serve as background material for readers of this book and does not claim to be a complete history of The Christian Community in the UK, nor of Evelyn's life. It has been compiled from various sources, including the Rudolf Steiner House library in London. Because of contradictory statements occurring in some of the available material, no claims to correctness are made.

Isla Bourke, October 1997

Appendix II

Evelyn Francis Capel's Writings

A record of the Books, Pamphlets and Typescripts written by Revd Evelyn Francis Capel, BA (Oxon.), FRSA (Fellow of the Royal Society of Arts). Her maiden name was Francis; her first married name was Derry.

Out of print books can be borrowed from:

(a) the Library at Rudolf Steiner House, 35 Park Road, London NW1 6XT
(b) The Christian Community (London West), Temple Lodge, 51 Queen Caroline Street London W6 9QL.

The main publishers are:	*Abbreviations used*
The Christian Community (London West)	CC London West,
Temple Lodge	or TL Press, or
51 Queen Caroline Street	TL Publishing
London W6 9QL	
The Christian Community	CC London NW3
34 Glenilla Road	
London NW3 4AP	
Floris Books	Floris
15 Harrison Gardens	
Edinburgh EH11 1SH	

Books and Pamphlets

Year	Title and Publisher
1949	*Seven Sacraments in the Christian Community* CC London NW3; reprinted 1982 by Floris
1951	*Thinking about Christianity* CC London NW3
1964	*Growing Up in Religion* CC London NW3; reprinted in 1992 as *The Mystery of Growing Up* by TL Publishing
1967	*The Christian Year* CC London NW3; reprinted 1982 and 1991 by Floris
1969	*A Self-Portrait of Christ* CC London West
1970	*Man's Development Foreseen in Goethe's 'Faust'* (pamphlet, 14th Foundation Lecture) New Atlantis Foundation
1975	*The Timeless Storyteller* CC London West; revised edition 1995 by TL Publishing
1976	*The Tenth Hierarchy* TL Press

1976	*Glossary for German and English Terms in Anthroposophy* (with P. Kipfer) Philosophisch-Anthroposophischer Verlag, Dornach
1978	*Birth* TL Press; reprinted 1987 by TL Press
1979	*Festivals in North and South* Floris
1979	*Death: The End is the Beginning* TL Press; revised edition 1990 as *Understanding Death* by TL Press
1980	*In the Midst of Life* TL Press
1980	*The Making of Christianity and the Greek Spirit* Floris
1981	*Studies in Christian Meditation* TL Press
1983	*The Reappearing of Christ* Floris
1985	*The Creed in The Christian Community* (pamphlet) Floris
1988	*Marriage* TL Press
1988	*Reincarnation within Christianity* TL Press
1989	*Christ in the Old and New Testaments* (with Alfred Dowuona Hammond) TL Press
1989	*An Introduction to Counselling* TL Press
1989	*Pictures from the Apocalypse* TL Press
1990	*Understanding Death* TL Press (first published in 1979 as *Death: The End is the Beginning*)
1991	*Celebrating Festivals around the World* TL Publishing
1992	*The Mystery of Growing Up* TL Publishing (reprint of the 1964 *Growing Up in Religion*)
1992	*Prayers and Verses for Contemplation* Floris
1992	*Collected Plays for Young and Old* TL Publishing
1992	*A Woman in the Priesthood* TL Publishing
1993	*Towards Freedom: A Journey of Discovery through Rudolf Steiner's 'The Philosophy of Spiritual Activity'* TL Publishing
1997	*The Celtic Inheritance in Christianity* Etheric Dimensions Press (Mull)
undated	*Festivals and Seasons* (pamphlet, reprinted from *The Christian Community* Vols. 1959 and 1960)

Unpublished Works
Helping the Dead
Relationships: You, I and We
These and various articles and other papers are currently held by: Miss S. C. Parton, 1 Ennerdale Road, Kew, Richmond, Surrey TW9 3PG.

Typescripts
The Library at Rudolf Steiner House holds a number of Revd Capel's typescripts on a variety of subjects related to The Christian Community and anthroposophy. Items 2 and 4 are also available at The Christian Community (London West). (The addresses of both these centres are on page 172.)
1. 1952-55: *Talks* (volumes 1–4)
These include Revd Capel's *Talks on Christian Relationships*, illustrated from the *Second Mystery Play* by Rudolf Steiner.

2. 1957: *Talks* (volume 5)

These include *Seasons and Festivals: Studies in the Spiritual Significance of the Seasons of the Year and the Christian Festivals from Ideas given by Rudolf Steiner* (in 9 parts): These were produced when The Christian Community (London West) was located at Benen House, Chelsea, London SW3.

3. 1960: *The Three Maries*: A Play

4. 1968: *Stress: A Dialogue between Evelyn and Guy* (with G. Wint) – article in *Theoria to Theory* Vol.2, 2nd quarter, Jan.)

For many years Revd Capel's *Companions/Letters on the Inner Life* were circulated to members of The Christian Community. In 1994 she started a new series. Interest has been expressed in seeing these series published in their entirety.

September 1997

Index of Contributors

Adcock, Barbara 66–68
Aegler, Regula and Roland 123
Allan, Revd Peter 123–124
Andriesse, David 68
Anon 1 37
Anon 2 117
Anthony, Kathleen 102
Armstrong, Julian 68–69
Avison, Kevin 124–125
Bana, Aban 37–38
Bayfield, Audrey 38–40
Beaumont, Michael 125–127
Bell, Revd Allan 69
Bourke, Isla 69–71
Bridgmont, Peter 127
Bryan, Oda Thekla 102–103
Burchard, Dr Otto and Gertrude 104
Campbell, John 40–41
Carter, Christine 91–92
Castle Stewart, The Earl Pat 71–72
Collins, Alan 57–59, 72–73
Croasdell, Amy 92–94
Da Deppo, Judith 41–42
Daunt, Margaret 127–128
Davies, Susan 94–95
De Bruyne, Nim 95
Donnithorne, Ruth 42–43
Dorrell, John 73–74
Dostal, Revd Jan 23–26
Drummond, Michael 43–45
Edmonds, Renate 74–75
Ellis, Irene 45
Filon, Lisa 75
Fisher, Cecelia 13–22
Fisher, Jacqui and Martin 95–96
Flanagan, Elizabeth 128–131

Flynn, John 131–132
Forge, Lily 75–77
Furst, Dr Branko 96–97
Gibbons, Ivan 46
Gilmer, Virginia 77
Goodman, Dorothy 77–78
Gulbekian, Sevak 117–118
Hall, Peggy 118–119
Hammond, Alfred Dowuona 78–80
Hartley, Eileen 105
Heathfield, Peter 46–47
Helfgott, Gillian 47–48
Hereford, Berenice 132–133
Himstedt, Revd Franz-Heinrich 26–28
Hoerner, Revd Wilhelm 28–29
Hugo, John 59–61
Jones, Edna 81
Karnes, Alice Barton 133–134
Kassner, Bernd 134–135
Kirst, Rudolf 105–106
Koenig, Julian 81–82
Langston, Paul 135–136
Lauppe, Christiane and Michael 97
Lawrie, Charles 136–138
Lees, John 82–85
Leingang, June 85–86
Lewis, Margaret Gwyneth 48–49
Luxford, Jane 139
Macniven, Shireen 49–50
Maestrini, Joan 86
Mainstone, Rhoda 139–140
March, Cath 86–88
Marcus, Joan 140
Marquardt, Ursula 140–141

Mellor, Patricia and Harold 50–51
Milne, William 141–143
Mirman, Dr Jacob 143
Montague, Brid 143–145
Mooney, Diane 145–147
Napper, Muriel 147
Newman, Dr Michael 51–52
Nightingale, John 29–32
Nimmo, Maria 147–148
Nosek, Milena and Libor 106–107
Oduro, Charles Edward 107–112
Oliveriusová, Eva 112
Padday, Mollie 148–149
Page, Stuart 61–62
Parker, Cynthia 149–151
Parton, Stella 119–120
Pears, Pat 151
Percival, Dorothy 151–152
Poer, Nancy 112–113
Quanjer, Johan Henri 153
Rauter, Claire 153
Reid Jones, Janet 88–89
Rodriguez Hart, Dyana 97–98
Samuel, Beatrice 98–99

Sleigh, Revd Julian 113–116
Smirthwaite, William 120
Storr, Elizabeth 154
Straker, Hazel 154–155
Taylor, Valerie 52–53
Thomas, Ann 155–156
Thomson, Anne 32–34
Toms, Julie and Arbel, Neil 99–101
Tonge, Julia 89–90
Turner, Margaret 90
Twamley, Olive and Jim 156–157
Tweedale, Fiona 62–64
Voigt, Revd Walther 36
Walsh, Ann 53–56
Weber, Gabriele 157–158
Welziel, Elizabeth 90
Wessling, Maria Fernanda and Fritz 116
White, Alan 121
Willby, Nelson 121–122
Williams, Dr Basil 158–160
Williams, Christina 160–164
Woollven, Nicholas 164–166